Building Your Own
Climbing Wall

Building Your Own Climbing Wall

Illustrated Instructions and Plans for Indoor and Outdoor Walls

Steve Lage

GUILFORD, CONNECTICUT
HELENA, MONTANA
AN IMPRINT OF ROWMAN & LITTLEFIELD

FALCONGUIDES®

Copyright © 2012 Steve Lage

FalconGuides is an imprint of Rowman & Littlefield.

How to Climb, Falcon, FalconGuides, and Outfit Your Mind are registered trademarks of Rowman & Littlefield.

Photos and illustrations by Steve Lage unless noted otherwise.

Distributed by NATIONAL BOOK NETWORK

Library of Congress Cataloging-in-Publication Data
Lage, Steve.
    Building your own climbing wall : illustrated instructions and plans for indoor and outdoor walls / Steve Lage.
        p. cm. — (How to climb)
    Includes bibliographical references and index.
        ISBN 978-0-7627-8023-5 (alk. paper)
    1. Climbing gyms. 2. Indoor rock climbing. I. Title.
        GV200.2.L34 2012
        796.522'3—dc23
                                                                        2012019191

Printed in the United States of America

Contents

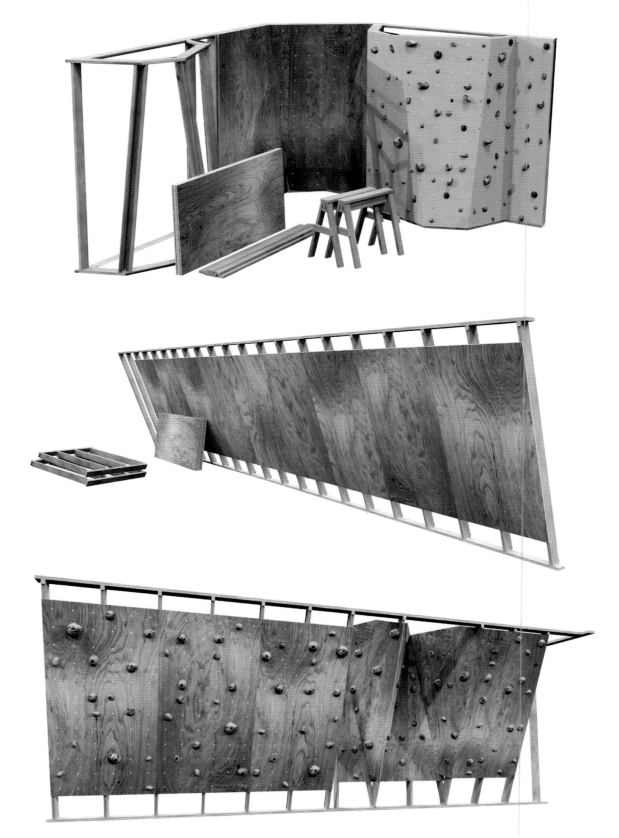

CHAPTER 1

Why Build a Climbing Wall?

If you want to get a total body workout, climbing is the way to do it. You will exercise your mind with problem-solving skills, and your endurance, strength, and both the fast and slow twitch muscles with the physical skills required in climbing. The best part is that climbing will keep you interested. While working out at a fitness center can be monotonous, working out on a climbing wall is always new. Climbing provides its own motivation. You will get a sense of satisfaction and accomplishment by working toward, then finally mastering, difficult problems. Climbing will help you improve the physical, mental, and social aspects of your life. It's hard to find a better sport.

With your own rock-climbing wall, you will get:

- Both aerobic and anaerobic exercise
- A thorough workout for a wide and diverse set of muscles
- Enjoyable problem-solving challenges
- A place for trust building, camaraderie, and self-confidence
- A great place for teens to spend time
- A pleasurable setting for parties or small groups of friends

As an exercise, you really can't do better than climbing. Climbing will improve all aspects of your physical condition. You will see improvement in your balance, flexibility, and agility and develop both upper and lower body strength. Best of all, you will burn calories at a higher rate than with most strenuous workouts and will do it before you know it. Climbing burns about 500 to 700 calories per hour depending on your weight and how strenuously you work out. With climbing as an exercise, you have a lot to gain (or should I say lose?).

Indoor climbing as an activity is growing at about 18 percent per year. As of early 2012 there were about 3,000 indoor climbing gyms worldwide listed at Indoorclimbing.com. Based on the growth of the listing itself, indoor climbing facilities have increased in number at about 12 percent per year. There is no doubt indoor climbing has become a popular sport in its own right.

The size and shape of artificial climbing walls are limited only by one's imagination. Creative people are building artificial climbing walls in the most unusual places. Here are some of the highest and most unusual artificial climbing walls:

1. The Luzzone Dam in Ticino, Switzerland, holds the record for the highest artificial climbing route in the world. It has one route that is 738 feet long and composed of about 650 holds.

Your own climbing gym will give you a great workout, and it can also become an enjoyable gathering place where active people can socialize.

2. The second-highest is the Emosson Dam located near Chamonix, France. It has a single route that's 387 feet in length.

3. The outdoor Base Camp Climbing Wall in Reno, Nevada, is an impressive 164 feet high. It also boasts a massive 7,000-square-foot indoor bouldering park featuring 2,900 square feet of climbable area.

4. The Excalibur is a 121-foot-high dedicated outdoor climbing structure located in Groningen in the Netherlands. This impressive structure is located in front of the Klimcentrum Bjoeks climbing gym.

It's clear that climbing is continuing to increase in popularity, and why not? It is an excellent, exhilarating exercise that fosters trust, confidence, and social interaction. For just a few hundred bucks, careful planning, and some time, you can have the satisfaction, pride, and immediate access to your very own climbing wall.

Climbing is great exercise. You will burn 500 to 700 calories per hour and work both strength and endurance simultaneously.

CHAPTER 2

Building a Climbing Wall Step-by-Step

Building a climbing wall can be an enjoyable and rewarding experience. It doesn't have to be a high or complicated wall—you'll get an excellent workout on a slightly overhung, straight floor-to-ceiling wall, and the typical ceiling height of a home is just right for a great climbing wall. This book will give you ideas and building tips, along with methods that have worked for many other climbers. While you are getting your ideas together, visit indoor climbing gyms and pay particular attention to the shapes and sizes of the walls. Gather your ideas and begin planning your project.

Step 1:
Planning and Designing Your Wall

The first and most important step in the process is planning. In fact, you need to plan to plan. Set the time aside for this important first step. Using your training goals, the planning process will end with a workable concept sketch and 3-D model. The sketch and model will help you develop a materials list and equipment list. This book will show examples and walk you through the planning, design,

and building process. If you set out to do this in a methodical and systematic way, you will end up with a really nice home climbing wall.

Ben Franklin said, "If you fail to plan, you plan to fail." If there's one thing you should get out of this section, it is to take the extra time required for careful planning. The very first thing to do is decide what type of climber you are or what aspect of your climbing you want to improve.

Define your Training Objectives

You may know where you want to improve, or you may know the type of climbing you will be doing. Various features on a climbing wall will require you to master a particular skill. So if you want to improve in a certain area, make yourself a climbing wall with the features that require that skill set.

Here are common climbing wall features, with the corresponding skills needed for those features.

VERTICAL OR NEAR VERTICAL WALLS

Vertical walls are good for beginning climbers, but advanced climbers can gain a lot from this type of wall too. Anyone wanting to improve endurance,

Your climbing wall doesn't need to have a complex design. If you are ready to build your first wall or need to keep costs down, simple is always better. You'll still get a great deal of benefit from a basic climbing wall design.

Vertical or near vertical walls provide an endurance workout. Features and texture add interesting shapes.

©YANLEV / LICENSED BY SHUTTERSTOCK.COM

Moderate overhangs are perfect for practicing dynamic movement like lunges and dynos.

balance, lock-offs, cross-throughs, gastons, sidepulls, flagging, matching hands or matching feet, high steps, backsteps, and toe pulls will benefit from working out on vertical walls. With interesting features, ledges, and protrusions added, vertical walls can be made challenging for experienced climbers as well as beginners. For children the lower sections can be built with a nearly vertical or even positive incline. The higher sections can be overhung with smaller holds for advanced climbers to use. A vertical wall will provide excellent climbing for young kids, as well as novice and more advanced adult climbers alike.

MODERATELY OVERHANGING WALLS

Dynamic movement, like dynos and lunges, can be practiced best on walls with a moderate overhang. Training to improve dynamic movement does not require features or texture. This type of overhang uses a great deal of upper body strength and will help improve those muscles. Climbing moves like the kneedrop and heel hook can be improved on a moderately overhanging wall.

STEEP OVERHANGING WALLS

A steep overhanging wall will help you focus on improving your upper body strength and torso, back, and leg strength. The most effective training on this type of wall is short bursts of maximum exertion in two or three sets. You don't need height or distance. All you need is enough space to do a circuit on a steep overhang. You can learn or improve swinging the lower body from left to right as you move your feet from hold to hold. This movement will completely change your orientation on the wall. Heel hooks can also be practiced on steep overhanging walls. Roof, cave, and overhead climbing can be improved with steep overhanging walls, and these walls can also help you improve your ability to use and stick underclings. Undercling holds are usually placed lower relative to the foot position. This type of hold uses an entirely different set of muscles. If you need practice with underclings, a steep overhanging wall will help. Be aware that a steep overhang does require more floor area for the fall zone than other types of climbing walls.

Height of the Wall

Usually home climbing wall heights are limited by the ceiling. From about the end of World War II to the mid-1990s, the standard home ceiling height was 8 feet. In the mid- to late 1990s, builders began constructing 9-foot ceilings. Pre–World War II homes and some of the newer high-end homes have 10- and 12-foot ceilings. Basement ceiling height, or basement joist height, is usually around 7 feet. Basement heights vary from place to place and builder to builder.

Appendix D contains a handy chart to determine the run (distance from the wall) required to achieve a particular angle for the most common ceiling heights. The ceiling height is the rise, and the distance from the wall is the run. For example, if you have a 9-foot ceiling and you want a 30-degree overhanging angle, find the 9-foot column, then find the 30-degree angle. Read the "run" to the right. In this example the run is 62¼ inches. In other words, the inclined climbing panel will anchor to the 9-foot ceiling at 62¼ inches from the wall to form a 30-degree angle at the base. The trig formula for this is "run = rise times that tangent of the incline angle."

What if Your Purpose Is Purely Recreational?

If your purpose for building a climbing wall is purely recreational, you may want to incorporate several vertical sections, a moderately overhanging section, and a steeply overhanging ledge transitioning between them. Be creative and include features such as caves, stalactites, columns, and arêtes to add interest and wow your guests. A training wall may not need many features to meet its intended purpose, but as long as the features do not inhibit training, there is no reason to leave them out.

Overhanging walls provide excellent strength and power training.

Step 2:
Making a Sketch and a Model

After you decide what type of climbing wall you need, start sketching the ideas and concepts that have the features you want. The purpose of sketching is to help you define the overall shape. After revisions the sketch will serve as a construction blueprint with dimensions, measurements, and assembly notes listed on it. It should contain all the details of the cuts and individual piece sizes.

As you plan your project, make sure you have enough space to actually assemble it and that you have a large enough fall zone.

When you start out, the sketch will be a simple overview of the entire wall. However, you can continue to make smaller sketches of smaller sections. Make adjustments to your plan as you go. It will evolve into a firm concept with height, length, width, and overhang angle.

If you have access to design software, you may prefer to do the drawing on your computer.

Whether by hand or by computer, your sketch should have all dimensions labeled. Record distances

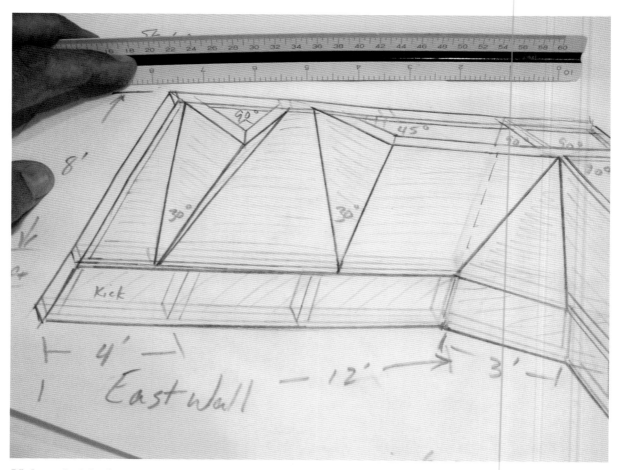

Make a sketch of your concept. Get the big-picture ideas down on paper.

from the climbing wall to the house walls and ceiling. Label the distances of studs and joists, which are behind the sheetrock. You also need to locate the electrical lines and any other cables or objects in the wall or ceiling before attaching anchors. Get up in the attic and check above the ceiling to locate and verify electrical lines or other utility lines.

You can use a stud finder to locate studs in the walls and ceiling. A stud finder measures relative density. Try it a few times to make sure you are getting a consistent reading. It will sound a beep and a red light will come on when it senses a change in density.

As you dimension your wall, be aware that the designated size of US lumber is not the same as its actual thickness. US lumber is designated by its *nominal value*. When lumber is milled, it is first cut to the actual size, which is also called the nominal size. The nominal size of a 2 x 4 is 2 inches by 4 inches. After the lumber is cut, it is planed and sanded. This finishing process removes ¼ inch from both dimensions. So the finished size of a 2 x 4 is actually 1½ inches by 3½ inches. Be sure to account for the difference in finished size due to the final sanding and finishing at the mill.

Utility lines in the attic are often close to the beams and joists. Make sure you climb up and visually check for clearance before cutting or drilling.

A stud finder is used to locate the stud behind the sheetrock.

(Plywood is not milled, so the final size of a 4 x 8 x ¾-inch sheet of plywood is actually that size.)

While you are forming the concept and being creative, keep in mind that you need to be able to build the framework so it forms a continuous load path to the floor. A continuous load path is a term used to describe the distribution of the force of the weight of the wall and the live loads from the climber(s) from the top overhanging section to the floor. Do not hesitate to seek professional design help if you feel you cannot do this.

Using the information you have gathered and the sketch with dimensions, create a scale model. The model can be made with an inexpensive material like poster board, construction paper, cardboard, or even balsa wood. Choose a convenient scale to use. If you are working in feet and inches, a good scale might be 1 inch = 1 foot. So, if your garage walls are 9 feet high, your model will be 9 inches high. If are working in metric units, you will have the convenience of using decimal divisions. A scale plan based in metric units would transfer to the construction process easily. Most tape measures today also have metric units.

Don't be tempted to skip making the model. With a sketch that is labeled and dimensioned, it may seem like you are ready to buy lumber and start building. However, climbing walls are three-dimensional, while your drawings are two-dimensional. A little extra time put into a model will do a lot of good.

Here are some of the benefits of making a scale model:

1. **Visualization.** In the planning stages, a three-dimensional model is a very good way to develop the overall conceptual plan to build the climbing wall. The model helps you visualize the three-dimensional structure you are about to build.

2. **Streamline construction.** By cutting out rectangular pieces to represent the plywood sheets, you intuitively develop your construction sequence. It is much better to do this on inexpensive materials rather than expensive plywood and lumber. You may find that a plywood piece cannot span both the length and width you planned. Your model will help refine the details of the concept and may highlight some conceptual flaws that you might not have otherwise noticed. It's much less expensive to fix a problem before your lumber is cut.

3. **Verify constructability.** In commercial construction projects the design firm holds constructability reviews. They bring in experts from all major trades. These individuals are usually unfamiliar with the project, so they look at the plans and specifications with fresh eyes. The purpose is to determine if it can be built as designed. Use your model to think through the assembly of the project. Building a model is like a constructability review, helping you conceptualize the construction sequence and find and correct problems before they happen.

Step 3: Gathering Materials and Tools

Make a list of materials that includes prices (see example on page 63). Use the model, your sketch, and measurements taken from your work area and determine the materials you will need. Transfer all your materials to a spreadsheet. Create two or three columns for pricing items at several stores. When you finish planning and you're ready to move on to construction, print the list and take it with you to two or more lumberyards or hardware stores. Fill in the prices in the two columns corresponding to each store. On the spreadsheet, set up a formula to add each column, and one to add only the lowest price from either column. This will give you the pricing information you need to choose the store with the lowest overall cost, or the lowest cost between two stores.

Start a list of tools at the same time you start your materials list. When you add an item to the materials list, think through the task required to use that item and the tool or tools required. Write the tool name down as soon as you think of it. Here are the common tools used for building a climbing wall:

✓ Circular saw

✓ Chop saw or miter saw

✓ Drill with Phillips bit attachment

✓ 4-foot level

✓ Chalk line

✓ Tape measure

✓ Framer's pencils

✓ Extension cords

✓ Gloves, safety goggles, earplugs

✓ Framing square

✓ Stepladder

✓ Sawhorses

✓ Drop cloth, roller, roller frame, 5-gallon bucket

- ✓ Roller screen, paintbrushes
- ✓ C clamps and wood clamps
- ✓ 7⁄16-inch spade-type drill bit for T nuts
- ✓ Hammer
- ✓ Tool belt
- ✓ String
- ✓ Laser level
- ✓ Stud finder
- ✓ T bevel

Keeping Costs Down

SIMPLICITY OF DESIGN

A complex design may require additional support structure, may take longer to build, and adds much more potential for errors in design or construction, all of which drive costs up. A straightforward design that is easy to understand and build will be the most cost effective—as long as it meets your needs.

SMART SHOPPING

Having a plan laid out is the key to buying your materials at good prices. If you stick with the plan, you will know the materials you need to buy, but if you build and design as you go, you will buy countless extra and unneeded items. Follow your materials list when comparing prices.

Cull Bin Option

When you're at the lumberyard, ask to check out the cull bin. A cull bin is a collection of scraps that lumberyards may sell at significantly reduced prices. Usually these scraps are high-quality lumber pieces that are marked down simply due to their odd sizes.

Here are ten ways to shop smart and save money:

1. **Use your materials list as a shopping list.** Make several columns for cost comparisons between different stores. Visit several stores and write down the cost of the items you will need in the column for that store. You don't have to buy all materials from the same store.

2. **Use the Internet.** There are several excellent online climbing gear retail stores that hold semiannual and micro sales throughout the year. You can get deals on climbing holds, T nuts, bolts, and wrenches. Visit indoorclimbing.com/compare to find the best price. It enables you to compare costs between multiple online vendors simultaneously.

3. **Don't rush.** Your climbing wall will be with you for years to come. Take your time, plan carefully, and wait for deals.

4. **Keep your work area clean and organized.** This may sound trivial, but you will drive up your construction time and possibly your costs if you cannot find tools or a particular structural piece when you need them.

5. **Use coupons.** The Sunday paper is a great source for sale flyers and coupons. Check hardware stores and lumberyards, and take your materials list with you for cost comparisons. You can shop online for climbing and bouldering gear using coupons at indoorclimbing.com/coupons.

6. **Check pawn shops.** It's hard to justify a full-price tool you will only use for one or two projects. Pawn shops often offer deals on perfectly working tools at up to 50 percent off the price of new ones.

7. **Rent tools rather than buying.** Most hardware stores or major lumberyards have tools for rent. Renting is much less expensive than purchasing a rare tool for a single use.

Gather materials and tools in one location. Lay everything out in plain view for easy inventory.

8. **Check auction websites.** This is another source for used tools and is a good way to save money. Use caution when buying used gear or materials.

9. **Visit local secondhand stores.** Local stores may have even better deals than online auctions simply because they have a limited customer base.

10. **Use rough-cut lumber.** The finish quality of the lumber used doesn't need to be top grade. CDX plywood and other rough-cut lumber is much less expensive. After all, if it is desirable to have micro features on a climbing surface, why pay for top-grade finished plywood to get a mirror-smooth surface, especially if you plan on using texture? Texture will cover a multitude of sins, such as bumps, holes, and imperfections in the wood.

Building Permits, Zoning, and Community Covenants

Permits apply to construction standards and safety. Zoning applies to the type of use. Your community's "covenants, conditions, and restrictions" (CC&R) apply to community standards. If your personal climbing wall is in your home and does not alter the structure of the existing facility, most likely it will not require a building permit, zoning consideration, or approval from a homeowners association.

The requirement for a building permit is definitely something to verify. It just takes a phone call to your city planning office. Usually you will need a building permit if you plan to modify the existing structure as part of the climbing wall construction. For example, anchoring to a wall using a ledger board may require a permit. Requirements vary from city to city.

For outdoor climbing walls the situation is a little different. If you need to dig down to anchor the wall, this usually requires a digging permit. If the wall is over 8 feet in height, it may require a permit and may also require a fence. CC&Rs may also apply to outdoor climbing walls to comply with community appearance standards.

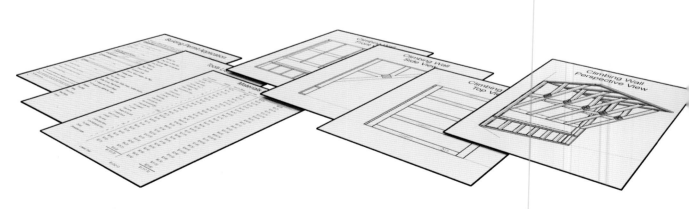

Step 4:
Constructing Your Climbing Wall

It's a lot of fun to put a careful plan and design together and see it taking shape. Construction of any climbing wall will have common basic principles. If you are not familiar with the construction terminology used here, refer to appendix B, Common Construction Terms.

Get the project started by organizing the lumber, tools, and materials. With the planning, drawings, and dimensioning done, you are ready to begin assembling the sections of the wall. Begin assembly by setting up the anchoring system.

A. Anchoring the Wall

There are several ways to anchor the climbing wall to the existing structure. You can anchor from the wall to the ceiling or from the floor to the ceiling. The anchor is the point where the weight of the climbing wall transfers to the house.

ANCHORING TO A FRAMED WALL

When anchoring to an existing wall, you will need to install a ledger board to bear the load or weight of the climbing wall. The ledger board must be capable of supporting the full weight, including the dynamic live loads created by the force of climbers moving on the wall. If you are not familiar with construction techniques, don't hesitate to hire a local expert who can install this critical support element. As installation of a ledger board may require a city permit, check with your city planning office to determine if a permit is necessary. The ledger anchor serves the same purpose and is constructed in the same way as the ledger for a deck built onto the exterior of a house.

The ledger board should be 6 to 8 inches wide depending on the size and angle of the studs. The end of the ledger should attach to a house wall stud and extend beyond the climbing wall. Use a 4-foot level or laser level to mark the top edge of the ledger on the wall. In most municipalities the building code will require you to install the ledger directly to the house wall studs. Therefore, if your garage's or basement's existing wall has sheetrock installed, you will need to cut out a section so the ledger can be mounted directly to the studs. Again, this depends on the building code in your area.

Temporarily tack the ledger board in place with two nails. Fasten the ledger to the wall using lag screws by drilling pilot holes into the wall studs at 2 inches from the top and bottom of the ledger board. Do not countersink the lag bolts. Screw each lag screw into the wall tightly using a socket wrench. Be careful not to overtighten and strip the wood around the threads.

The studs of the climbing wall attach to the ledger board with joist hangers, so they should not line up with the studs in the wall.

ANCHORING TO A CONCRETE WALL

Using a hammer drill and masonry bit, pre-drill holes according to the manufacturer's specifications. Usually it's about a ½ inch deeper than the depth the anchor will go. Align the hole in the ledger board to the hole in the concrete with a sixteen-penny nail, a screwdriver, or any long object. Press the ledger tight and remove the nail. Install the expansion anchors.

Use a drop-in concrete expansion anchor for fastening the climbing wall to a concrete wall or floor.

Note: Some types of masonry and hollow concrete-block walls cannot support an expansion anchor; therefore a ledger cannot be used. Check with your city building and inspections department.

ANCHORING TO THE FLOOR

Wear ear and eye protection when installing concrete anchors as the anchors may break. Set the bottom plate in place. Mark and drill the hole in the bottom plate. Remove the bottom plate. Drill the hole in the concrete about a ½ inch deeper than the anchor will extend into the concrete. (Wrap a piece of tape around the drill bit to indicate the depth you want.) Raise and lower the bit to clear the dust from the hole. Set the bottom plate back in place. Slip a washer on the anchor and set it into the hole in the bottom plate. Use a hammer to set the anchor into the concrete. Use a socket wrench to screw the bolt into the expanding anchor. See Building a Small Garage Climbing Wall in chapter 4 for an example of installing a concrete expansion anchor.

B. Leveling the Wall

Your climbing wall needs to be level in order to construct and fit pieces together. A garage floor may not be level, and walls and ceilings, especially in older homes, may have shifted. However, the length of a climbing wall is more than the longest construction levels. Fortunately there are several alternative leveling methods to use. Each method has its advantages and disadvantages.

LASER LEVEL

There are many laser-leveling devices available. Laser devices project a light on the surface. If you position the device correctly, it will give you a very accurate vertical or horizontal reference line. Be aware that when any of these devices are not set level, the line will be skewed. Some devices have highly accurate leveling systems. Other laser-leveling devices have a simple bubble to provide horizontal or vertical reference.

The laser level projects a straight line of light across relatively long distances.

2 X 4 AND 4-FOOT LEVEL

This method is commonly used for leveling footers in exterior construction such as building sheds, decks, patios, and the like. You can also use a 1 x 4 or other straight construction wood. The level is placed on a piece of wood to extend the length of the 4-foot level. When leveling a set of points that are lower in elevation than the starting point, attach another piece at a 90-degree angle as shown at top of page 19. The vertical piece is cut to the desired change in elevation from the origin.

WATER TUBE LEVEL

If you need to level around a corner or cannot use either the laser or string level (see page 20) for some reason, this leveling method will work. Get a

Above—For short distances, set a level on boards.

Right— A water tube level is easy to make with a bucket, a clear flexible tube, and a short board.

Below—For leveling where a straight line cannot be obtained, such as around a corner or behind an obstacle, a water tube level is the way to go. Water in the tube will equalize. The waterline at the end of the tube will always be the same elevation.

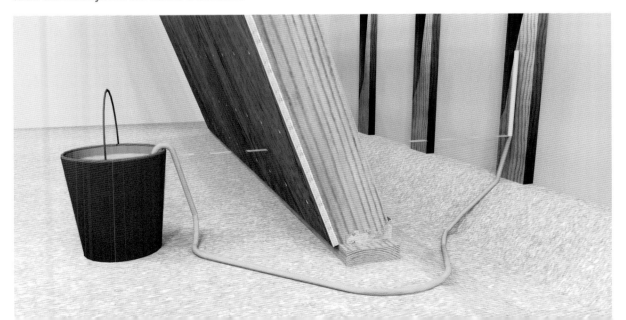

clear plastic flexible tube, a bucket, and something to fasten the tube to, like a board or pole. Fill the bucket with water. Tape one end of the tube to the board; place the other end in the bucket of water and start a siphon. Hold the tube above the water-line in the bucket to stop the flow of water. Mark the desired level point on the tube by placing it next to that point and allow the water to equalize in the tube. Then go to the location you want to level. Hold the tube up and let the water equalize again. The waterline in the tube will show you the level of the original point. Add a little dish detergent to the water to break the water tension and help the water move through the tube to equalize. You can also add a little food coloring to make it easier to see the waterline. After moving the end to a new location, the water will "bounce" up and down in the tube as it is equalizing. To help the water stabilize, pinch the tube slightly.

STRING LEVEL

This is a bubble level that attaches to a string. To use it, tack the string to the reference elevation. Then pull it out to the spot where you need to have the same reference elevation. Mark the midpoint between the origin and the place being leveled. This is the location to place the string level. The string level will slide along the string. Clip it onto the string and fix the end to the spot to be leveled. Check the bubble. Move the leveling spot up or

down until you have a level bubble. *Note:* This will not give an accurate reading if the bubble level is not centered halfway between the two spots.

C: Constructing the Framework

Each section of the framework should be made separately from the anchor and structural support trusses. In most cases the climbing wall should be constructed with 2 x 6 framing. While 2 x 4 framing might be sufficient for small modular sections that tie into the greater structure, 2 x 6 framing is best for forming the continuous load path from the top of the climbing wall to the floor. Do not hesitate to seek professional design help if you do not feel you can do this.

Screw the frame together using 3-inch screws. Do not use nails. The plywood sheathing lies over the framework and is also screwed to the frame. You can install the plywood sheathing to the framework before erecting the panel or after the framework is assembled in place. Either way, do not install the plywood until after the framework has been squared.

When laying out the frame, sight down the length of each beam. Check for a bend in the wood. All lumber will have a slight bend to it. Orient the joists so the bend, or crown, is up.

If the frame runs floor to ceiling, it should be assembled in place, not on the floor then lifted into place. The reason for this may not be apparent at

Place the level in the center of the string.

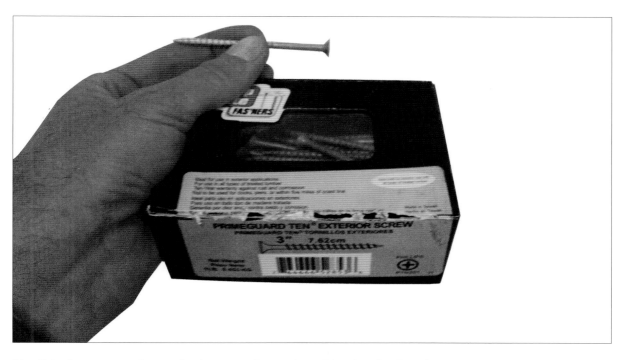

Use 3-inch screws to fasten the framework together. A 2 x 6 or 2 x 4 is 1½ inches thick. When the two are screwed together, the screw must go through the thickness of both, for a total length of 3 inches.

first. When installing a wall under a ceiling, a wall that is built exactly the same height as the ceiling will jam when you attempt to lift it from the floor and rotate it into place. This is because the distance between opposite edges of a frame (top front to bottom back) is greater than the length of the frame. Remodeling framers make their walls a little shorter, then shim the gap. This is not a good procedure for framing climbing walls. A climbing wall frame should fit securely with as little gap as possible.

If the frame is a small, modular section of a larger framework, it's easier to assemble it on the floor. To assemble a frame on the floor, you will start with the outer frame pieces. Just tack them together with small nails before you square the frame. This is done to keep the pieces from moving out of place as you make adjustments. Leave about ⅛ inch of the nailhead sticking up so you can remove these nails later.

Lay out the top and bottom plates. Mark the plates with the location of the studs. The end stud should be flush with the end of the plate. The second stud should be 15¼ inches from the end. The remaining studs will be 16 inches on center. The ¾-inch offset compensates for the first stud being aligned flush with the end. Make your measurements from the same side at the top and the bottom. Studs should all run in the same direction. Usually they are placed vertically.

Measure diagonally from opposite corners. Check the distance of both diagonals—they must be equal—and adjust accordingly. If the diagonal distances are not equal, the frame is not square. This method is far more accurate than trying to use a framing square. Recheck the square of the frame, then screw the frame together with 3-inch screws.

15¼"

16"

48"

Equal

Top—Check for a bend in the wood. All lumber will have a slight bend to it. Orient the joists so the bend, or crown, is up.

Bottom—Framing layout and squaring. Measure the diagonals and adjust the frame until the diagonals are equal. Assemble frames on the floor if they will be inserted as a modular section into a larger framework.

STRUCTURAL CONNECTORS

Structural connectors are hardware that connect the individual structural elements of your climbing wall to each other. Metal connectors increase the strength of joints and make the overall strength of a structure much greater than if the structural pieces were screwed directly together. They are commonly used in construction today to make homes and other structures more stable and secure from earthquakes and high winds. Connectors make framing easier and will add strength to the overall framework sustaining the climbing wall. They often can simplify the types of cuts or reduce or eliminate the need for some compound joints in connecting structural members. Connectors are not expensive in comparison to other aspects of a climbing wall. They are readily available and come in a variety of sizes and shapes. Here are some of the most common structural connectors for use in building a climbing wall.

Tie strap. This is a flat metal strap used in a similar way as the tie plate. A tie strap may be chosen over a tie plate due to its more convenient size.

Joist hanger. These are used in construction to attach a floor or ceiling joist to headers. The joist hanger can support an angled stud or joist. See Cutting Angled Joints on page 25 for how to fit a stud or joist at an angle.

A tie strap reinforces flat surfaces, functioning the same as a tie plate.

Two types of joist hangers are shown. The standard joist hanger on the left is more common and less expensive. The adjustable joist hanger on the right can be bent to fit angles up to 45 degrees and offers the additional flexibility to be skewed to either side to allow use of compound angles.

Framing angle. This is a versatile metal tie used in framing. It can be bent to match the required angle. However, as with any tie, only bend it once. Bending more than once weakens the joint.

Tie plate. These are flat metal plates with holes for screws. They reinforce flat surface joints. T connectors provide a similar function but can only be used when the joint is a T, whereas the tie plate can be used for any angle, and it's much less expensive.

Angle bracket or corner connector. This is a metal bracket designed to reinforce wood connections at 90 degrees.

A framing angle is bendable to allow adjustment to angles.

A tie plate reinforces flat surfaces.

An angle bracket, or corner connector, reinforces 90-degree angles.

D: Other Framework Construction Techniques

Whether constructing a wall with inclined sections or a more complicated climbing wall with irregular shapes, it's important to make the joints tight and flush. There are a few techniques and special tools available to help you measure and transfer angles to the wood members you need to cut. It's not difficult to measure and cut angles precisely, but it is an essential skill required for making tight strong joints.

CUTTING ANGLED JOINTS

For an inclined wall, it is not difficult to cut joists to fit joist hangers. Measure the angle you need using the angle finder, then transfer it to the T bevel. Cut the tip off the stud so it will fit into the joist hanger. Both the 2 x 6 and 2 x 4 joist hangers have a 2-inch tip. Using the T bevel and a framing square, mark the angle and the 2-inch tip at the same time.

Mark and cut the joist, and insert it into the joist hanger. Assemble the sections on the ground if they are small or modular sections of a larger framework. If the frame runs from floor to ceiling, the frame will need to be assembled in place.

Determine the location of the top plate using the Rise-Run chart in appendix D. Temporarily tack the top plate in place using screws or nails. Anchor the top plate to the ceiling joists using lag bolts. Anchor the bottom plate to the concrete floor using expanding anchor bolts. If the floor is wood, anchor it the same way as the ceiling top plate. Recheck the diagonals. When everything is aligned, screw the joists into the hangers. The easiest way to build an inclined wall is to make the entire length of the wall the same angle.

1) Transfer the angle to the T bevel.

2) Use the T bevel and framing square to mark the angled cuts to fit the joist hanger.

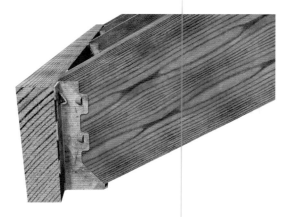

Above—This is an angled joint fitted to a joist hanger.

Left—A floor to ceiling frame is assembled in place. The top and bottom plates are anchored before the studs are attached.

Joists vs. Studs

In climbing wall construction the terms "joist" and "stud" are used interchangeably. In home construction a joist is a horizontal floor or ceiling structural member. A stud is a vertical framing member. Climbing walls are often angled, so sometimes there isn't a clear boundary between "mostly horizontal" and "mostly vertical." Therefore, these terms are used interchangeably here.

CREATING IRREGULAR SHAPES

Irregular shapes present a challenge to cut and fit accurately because they may not contain a right angle and/or may not have an edge parallel to the ground or parallel to any other edge on the climbing wall. They are created when two faces that are inclined vertically and angled on the horizontal plane meet. The gap between the two faces is the irregular shape. You will need to cut a plywood piece to fill into this space. Due to the irregular shape, it is sometimes difficult to cut a perfect fit.

To mark an irregular shape on plywood, start by measuring and recording the lengths of each of the sides of the irregular shape. On a sheet of plywood, draw a straight line the length of the first measurement. Starting on one of the ends of this line, draw an arc with a radius equal to the second measurement. On the other end of the line, draw another

arc with a radius equal to the third measurement. At the intersection of the first and second arcs, draw connecting lines to each end of the first line.

In the example below, two panels are inclined at about 20 degrees. The panel on the right is elevated 3 inches above the panel on the left. The lower transition panel's right side is 3 inches higher to meet the right base panel. This causes a small triangular void, which is indicated in yellow. Without a common parallel or right angle to the void, it can be tricky to cut a fitting piece. To mark and cut a piece to fit the void, measure all sides of the opening. On the sheet of plywood, pick a corner and side as a starting point.

In this example the bottom left corner is the starting point. Using a tape measure and carpenter's marking pencil, draw an arc from one of the corners at the distance measured along the bottom

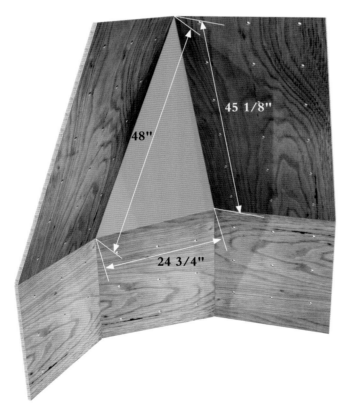

Irregular shapes are common in climbing walls.

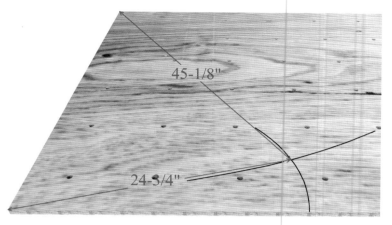

45-1/8"

24-3/4"

Measure all sides of the irregular shape you need to fill, then draw arcs from each corner with radius equal to a side. The intersection of the arcs will mark the corners of your shape. Connect each corner with a line and cut it out.

edge. From each end of the bottom edge, draw an arc at the distance of the connecting edge. The intersection of the two arcs is the third connecting point of the irregular shape.

Once you have marked the shape of the piece on the plywood, figure out what bevel angle to cut for each side of the triangle. The angle for the plywood joint is found by determining the dihedral angle.

CUTTING DIHEDRAL ANGLES

A dihedral angle is formed at the intersection between the two planes which are angled on both the horizontal and vertical planes. For overhanging walls the dihedral angle will be a little larger than the angle along the horizontal plane. Your climbing wall will have a nice professional appearance if you take just a little more time to get this angle right, and correctly set the bevel on your saw.

In the graphic at the top of page 29, the dihedral is shown by the blue line and the dihedral

angle is illustrated by the blue sweeping arrow. The horizontal plane is shown by the black dotted lines forming a 90-degree change in direction of the wall.

There are several ways to get the dihedral angle for the plywood joint. The easiest way is to measure the angle directly. There are several "angle-finder" tools available for this purpose.

Position the angle-finder tool to lie flush along both edges, and read the angle from the gauge. Make sure the angle finder is oriented at a right angle to the dihedral, not parallel to the ground. An angle finder will give you measurements for both an inside and outside angle. It is an excellent tool for sloped and compound angles and for reading any angle directly from the wall.

If you need to find the angle of an irregular shape that has not yet been installed, you can run a string from edge to edge and from the top to the bottom plate. This may give you the reference needed to get the measurement of the joint's angle.

Note: Since climbers are the target audience, let me make a quick clarification. A *dihedral* is also a term used by rock climbers to describe a rock formation in which two vertical rock faces come together to form a vertical corner. However, the term *dihedral,* as used in the context of design, is obviously not the rock formation. It is the angle formed by the intersection of two planes. In the case of a climbing wall, this would be the two sheets of plywood.

CUTTING COMPOUND ANGLES

Related to the dihedral angle is the compound angle. Geometrically speaking, they are the same. However, the "dihedral angle" is the term used to describe the line formed by two intersecting planes, in this case two climbing wall panels. When the term "compound angle" is used, people are usually referring to a type of cut requiring a bevel and miter adjustment.

To cut a compound angle, set the bevel and miter on the saw; see photos on page 30. A bevel refers to the tilt of the saw blade from the vertical axis. Furniture may have beveled edges to make it more comfortable, for example. A miter refers to the angle of the wood relative to the direction of cut, on the horizontal plane. For example, a picture frame is made with two 45-degree miter cuts to form a 90-degree angle. Therefore, a compound angle is created by cutting a bevel and miter at the same time.

The best tool to use for this type of cut is the chop saw, radial arm saw, or table saw. Each of these saws will allow you to set the bevel (tilt on the chop

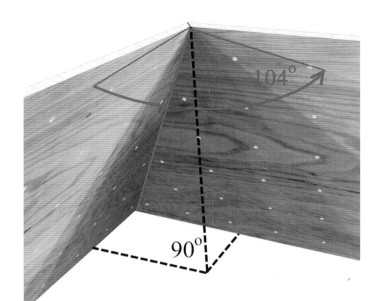

The dihedral angle and horizontal angle between two inclined planes is not equal.

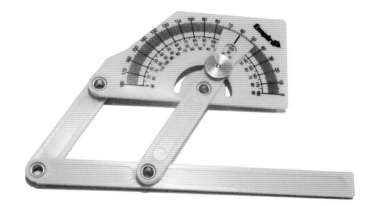

An angle finder will let you measure an angle directly. You'll need to know the angle measurement in order to set the bevel on the saw blade.

A chop saw can be adjusted to cut both the miter and bevel at the same time, creating a compound angle. This saw is tilted to cut a bevel and angled to cut the miter.

A compound angle is created when the angle of cut is in both the vertical and horizontal planes, or bevel and miter.

saw's blade creating the angle on the vertical plane) and the miter angle (the orientation of the wood relative to the direction of cut creating the angle on the horizontal plane).

E: Drilling T-Nut Holes

You will save a lot of time by drilling the T-nut holes all at once. Stack the sheets of plywood on sawhorses or a set of construction benches. The sheets should be face up (climbing side up) when you drill the holes. If you use low-grade CDX plywood, it probably doesn't matter which side you use to climb on. With the CDX grade, both sides are rough. If you have purchased plywood with one side finished to a higher quality, the finished side should face up. When the drill goes through the sheet, it will splinter a

little on the bottom side. By stacking them with the good side up, you will avoid creating splinters on the climbing side of the plywood sheets.

The easiest way to mark the grid is by using a chalk line. Measure and mark 4 inches from all sides, then every 8 inches to create an 8-inch grid.

If you are planning to use a cement texture, it's best to apply it after assembling the wall. The T-nut holes should be drilled after applying the texture, which means the holes must be drilled individually into the cement texture. If you are not planning on using texture, or if you are using a paint/sand or non-cement texture, you can drill the T-nut holes now or at any point before installing the plywood on the framework.

Stack the plywood sheets and clamp them together. Use a chalk line and mark the 8-inch grid. Drill through all sheets. This is much faster and reduces splintering on the bottom side of the sheets.

F: Installing T Nuts

After the support framework is constructed and the wall panel sections are framed, it's time to install the T nuts and then mount the plywood panels onto the frame. T nuts are installed in the plywood panels before mounting the panels to the frame but after cutting out any irregular shapes. It is much more difficult to install T nuts to a panel that is already in place. This is because you need to be able to pound the T nuts into the holes with a hammer. Pounding on a frame will weaken it. In addition the frame will absorb the force, making it even more difficult to seat the T nut.

Lay the plywood panels face down (intended climbing surface down). I take the extra time to put a drop of glue into the hole, then seat the T nut. This helps hold the T nut in the hole when you attach the first hold. Once the first hold is installed, the tightening of the hold will cinch the T nut further into the wood. It usually doesn't pop out after that.

Carefully hold the T nut and start it into the hole. Once it is started, a couple of solid and square hammer hits will be enough to seat it. Be careful not to hit off center. An off-center hit will make the T nut press into the hole at an angle. If this happens (and it will), pull it out with the claw of your hammer and try again. T nuts that are not squared up with the wood will be very difficult to thread a bolt into. When you install a hold, the bolt goes through the hold, then into the T nut. As a result you can't see the angle of the T nut in order to adjust the angle of the bolt. This is why it is difficult to thread if the T nut isn't seated squarely. Additionally, an angled T nut means that the back surface of the hold won't sit flush with the plywood panel. This condition will cause a spinner. So the best thing to do is just pull out an unsquared T nut as soon as it happens and try again.

Install T nuts from the back side of the sheet, with the climbing surface down. Do this before mounting the panel on the wall.

A drop of glue will hold the T nut in place until after the first hold is installed.

Make sure you seat the T nut square with the plywood panel. An unsquared T nut will be difficult to thread and may prevent your hold from seating flat against the panel.

SCREW-IN METHOD FOR INSTALLING T NUTS

The screw-in method is great for installing T nuts in a wall that is already in place. Some people prefer to apply texture first, then install the T nuts. Or if you need to repair a spinner, this is the method to use.

Thread the two nuts onto the threaded rod. Use two pliers to cinch the two nuts against themselves.

This holds the nuts in place, keeping them from traveling on the threads as the rod turns in the drill. The two washers provide a surface for the nuts to press against. The washers also press the climbing surface. If you have texture, avoid damage to it by adding a wood block to provide a larger surface area. For plywood climbing surfaces, the washers will suffice.

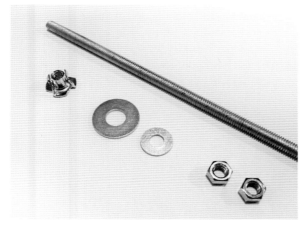

To make your own T-nut installer, buy a ³/₈-inch threaded rod, two nuts, and two washers.

Tighten two nuts against each other on the threaded rod. Tightening them against each other prevents them from traveling on the threads. Use washers to press against the nuts and climbing surface. For textured walls, add a block of wood so the washers do not damage the texture.

Clamp the drill's chuck onto the threaded rod. Carefully start the threads of the threaded rod with the T nut. Keep the drill speed slow so you have control.

Allow the T nut to tighten against the back of the panel until you can sense resistance. Reverse the drill to remove the threaded rod. Your T nut is now in place.

G: Installing the Panels and Sections

Assembling the wall can be done several ways, depending on the size and weight of the individual sections of wall. If your sections are small and modular in nature, you can mount the plywood sheathing on the framework on the ground, then fit each section into place on the wall. The problem with this approach is that it may make the sections heavy and difficult to maneuver. The advantage is that it is much easier to install small or irregularly shaped panels to a modular framework on the ground. If you have several people to help with the lifting, this might be the way to go. Large sections will be too heavy to lift into place with the plywood screwed on. For large sections, fasten the framework to the wall, then mount the plywood to the assembled framework.

Either way, when installing the panels, do not press the plywood tightly against an adjoining piece of plywood. Leave a very slight gap as plywood, like all wood, will expand and contract with humidity and temperature changes. This will ease the stress on the anchors, screws, and bolts holding the wall together.

With the climbing wall assembled and up, you can make some features from the scrap lumber and plywood. Rather than throw out the wood, why not put it to good use?

Step 5: Adding Features, Texture, and Holds

Adding climbing features will make your wall more interesting, add challenging obstacles, and make it more visually appealing. Features can be made with much of the scrap wood you will generate from the construction.

Adding Features

Odd small shapes are perfect for small and irregular features. Add internal bracing to hold the pieces together. In the example on the next page additional holes were drilled in plywood scraps, and T nuts were installed. Scrap 2 x 4s were cut at angles to support the plywood. The feature was then screwed into the plywood panel. Curved features make an attractive and effective training aid. Experiment with creating features. You have nothing to lose with scrap wood . . . except less to throw away.

The following photos show some examples of scraps being used to make features.

Protrusions and irregularly shaped features create interest and add potential for better training.

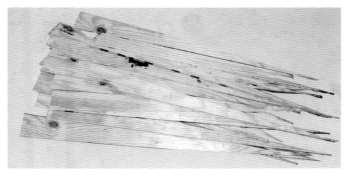

Keep scraps from the construction of your wall. In this example plywood triangles were left over from each panel section.

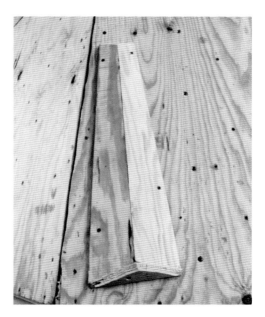

Cut wedges from 2 x 4s to make internal support for the feature.

Mount the feature on the wall at any angle or location. Screw it securely in place, making sure you hit joists.

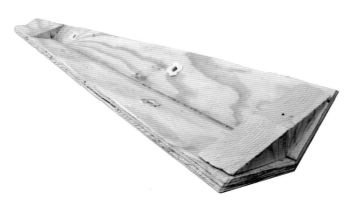

Install the T nuts in the plywood, then assemble the parts, fastening with screws and wood glue.

Fill gaps with texture. It may require several coats to smooth out the gaps.

A feature with a curved surface can easily be made by cutting grooves in the plywood. The grooves allow the plywood to bend in a uniform curve. A shape like this can be made any size. Start by cutting the shape and tapering the edges so that when curved, these edges will mount on the wall panel flat and securely.

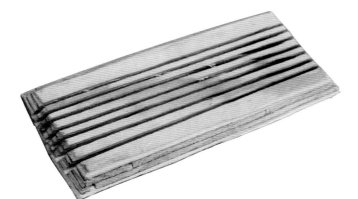

Cut grooves in the plywood. Set the depth of the saw to cut down to, but not into the bottom ply.

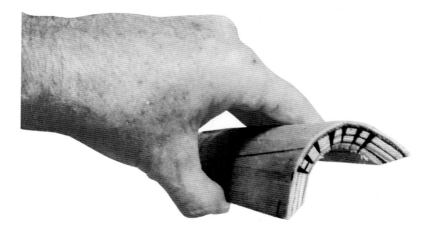

Soak the piece (or pieces) in water for about an hour, then slowly bend to the desired shape. Be careful not to let the outer ply break. You will hear a cracking sound if you bend it too far. Soaking longer will help it bend further.

Apply wood glue. Clamp or set the bent piece between blocks to keep it in the desired shape. Let it dry completely.

Mount the curved piece on the wall with screws. Larger curved features will need more backing than shown here.

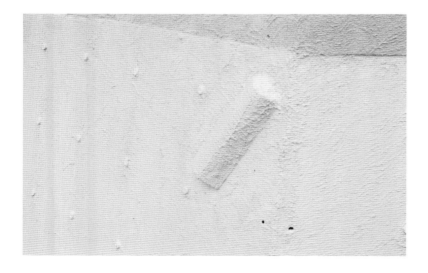

Texture will cover and fill gaps and imperfections.

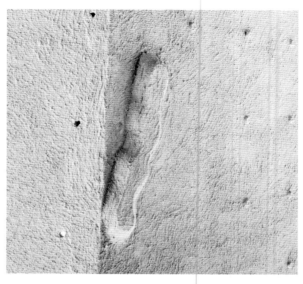

Scrap plywood can be cut in creative shapes and used as features. Features such as this can be useful for foot placement, sidepulls, or just to creatively add dimension and an attractive appearance to the wall.

Texture smooths out gaps but is not absolutely necessary on features. If you decide not to use texture but need to fill in gaps, a mixture of 90 percent wood filler and 10 percent wood glue will work pretty well. The wood filler provides the body to fill in small gaps but doesn't have strength by itself. Mixing in a little wood glue will bind it to the feature and help to keep it in place.

Creative shapes can be screwed anywhere on the wall.

Adding Texture

Often this step is omitted. You may find your climbing goals are met without using texture at all. If you decide to use texture, you have several options.

PAINT-AND-SAND TEXTURE

If you want texture but don't need a realistic look, a paint-and-sand mixture is easy to apply and works pretty well. Use silica sand for mixing directly with paint. This type of sand is clean and will give the best results.

Use a ratio of about four to one paint to sand by volume. However, experiment with ratios that give you the results you want. Sand settles to the bottom of the paint very quickly. Each time you dip the roller in the bucket, twist and plunge the roller to remix the sand and paint so the texture will be even.

The key to making a paint/sand texture work is to apply a final coat of paint (no added sand) over the paint/sand mixture. Without the final coat of paint, the sand tends to break off with a little pressure. The final coat of paint seals the texture and gives it the strength to withstand smearing.

All bare wood needs to be primed before applying texture. Primer helps to seal the wood, keeping moisture from working into the wood. It also bonds with the finish coat better than bare wood, making a more durable surface to climb on.

Texture Tip

Just a little drywall topping added to a paint-and-sand mixture will help suspend the sand. This will help keep it from sinking to the bottom of a bucket or roller pan. After applying the texture, let it dry, then apply a final coat of just paint.

TEXTURED PAINT

You can purchase a type of paint that creates texture as you roll it on. Designs can be added with a rag while the paint is still wet, or a trowel can be used to lightly knock down the peaks to give a textured look without roller patterns. This option will add small raised contours to your wall and offer a degree of friction for smearing. It will not have the same level of friction as sand, but it may be easier to apply.

CEMENT TEXTURE

Texture can be made with cement, plaster, stucco, or variations on these mixtures. Cement offers a realistic look and feel. Cement may have pigment or paint added to make the appearance more realistic.

There are disadvantages to using cement. The chemicals in cement can cause irritation to the skin if exposed to wet cement for long periods of time. And dry cement dust is hazardous to the eyes and lungs. Take precautions to avoid contact with the dust during mixing and skin contact during application. Take the time to look up the Material Safety Data Sheet for the particular cement product you are considering.

In addition to the toxicity hazard, cement is more difficult to apply than paint and more expensive per square foot. Cement must be applied with a trowel. This application method is already difficult, but it's made much more difficult if the T-nut holes are already drilled and plugged with golf tees sticking out (see Applying the Texture, page 42).

If you plan on applying cement as a texture, it is better to drill the T-nut holes *after* the cement dries and cures; this also means you have to drill each T-nut hole separately, rather than stack the sheets and drill through several sheets at a time.

POLYMER CEMENT ADDITIVES

Polymer additives create a latex when mixed with water. A polymer cement additive increases both the tensile (stretching) and flexural (bending) strength of cement. The result is a less brittle texture that stands up well to the slight bending of a climbing wall. Polymer cement additives are widely available at lumber and hardware stores.

MAKING A HOMEMADE, INEXPENSIVE, AND ENVIRONMENTALLY FRIENDLY TEXTURE

There are many combinations of materials that can be used as an aggregate and binder, which can be strengthened with a nontoxic glue.

First, consider the makeup of various cements:

- Plaster is a mixture of water and clay.
- Mortar is a mixture of water, clay, and sand.
- Cement is a mixture of water, clay, sand, and limestone.

- Concrete is a mixture of water, cement, and gravel.
- Stucco is made from water, cement, sand, and hydrated lime.

You can see that the cement variations are closely related. Their common components are (1) a structural filler, (2) a binding agent, (3) aggregate, and (4) water. Also notice that plaster and mortar do not have a binder. So, considering how these mixtures are made, it wouldn't be a big leap to make a homemade texture. Just find components that will act as the filler, binder, and aggregate, and of course, add water.

My Texture Experiment

Drywall topping. This is essentially a clay and serves as the structural filler. By itself it is not strong, just as plaster (clay and water) is not strong until sand and lime (the aggregate and binder) are added. Drywall topping will suspend the sand (keep it from sinking to the bottom of the bucket) and give the texture body.

Play sand. This is the aggregate. You could also use silica sand, but it is more expensive. Play sand is readily available at almost all discount department store chains. The fine size provides excellent friction, yet is not painful when you accidentally rub your knee or elbow against it.

Exterior primer-sealer. This is the binder. A water-based primer-sealer will mix well with the texture and when dry, serve to glue it all together.

The sand interlocks within the mixture and gives the texture strength. The primer-sealer binds or glues the mixture together. The drywall topping helps sus-

pend the sand and gives the mixture a little body. All that's left is to experiment with the ratio of the components. After a couple days of experimenting, here's what I came up with for my homemade texture ratio:

- One part joint compound
- Two parts water-based primer-sealer
- Three parts play sand
- Water

See the Building an Outdoor Climbing Wall section in chapter 4 for pictures of this texture in use. Experiment with a mixture that works for you. Some people may not want a sandy feel. Some may want more abrasion for smearing.

Suspending the Aggregate

The all-purpose joint compound does a very good job suspending the sand in the mixture. In other words the mixture at the bottom of the bucket has the same

The basic formula for any cement is binder, aggregate, and adhesive. There are many sources for each of these parts. The mixture pictured is joint compound, water-based primer-sealer, sand, and water. Use water-based products together, and use oil-based products together—don't mix them. If your paint and sealer is oil-based, or alkyd, then you will need to thin the mixture with mineral spirits rather than water.

Find a 1 x 2 or 1 x 3 piece of lumber and stir the three-part mixture thoroughly. The joint compound suspends the sand, preventing it from sinking to the bottom of the bucket. The primer-sealer provides a binder, gluing the mixture together. The sand provides the texture and helps improve strength by supplying an interlocking quality.

proportion of sand as the upper part of the mixture. You can see in the photo that the sand is not sinking to the bottom of the mixture. This is not true with the paint/sand texture described earlier. Without the all-purpose joint compound, you will have to stir the mixture before dipping the roller each time.

APPLYING THE TEXTURE

Before applying texture, take the added precaution to plug the T-nut holes, as both sand and the primer-sealer will make it very difficult to get the bolt for the holds to catch the threads. To protect your T-nut threads, you can plug the holes with golf tees.

Get the tees without a glossy coating. The glossy coating makes them so slick they won't stick in the T-nut holes. Unfinished wood or flat-painted tees will stick much better.

The package may not give that kind of information about the tee. Just look at it and see if there is a sheen to the surface of the tee. If it has a flat finish, or it's just plain wood, that is the kind of tee to get.

Once the T-nut holes are plugged, start painting the texture at the highest locations and work down. Apply the paint/sand texture with a roller in a lengthwise direction to the sheet sheathing. Apply the texture in one direction, then even out the roller marks by rolling at a 90-degree angle. With light pressure on the roller, go over the panel again in the original direction (lengthwise to the panel). For edges you will need to cut in with a paintbrush. Slap the brush lightly to get the paint/sand texture to come off the paintbrush.

The tees may pop out. If so, stop rolling on the texture and press the tee back into the hole. The texture does not glue them in place. They are easy to remove when it is time to do so.

Buy a bag of golf tees and put them in the T-nut holes. This will protect the threads from the paint and texture. Get cheap, unfinished or flat-painted tees. Do not get plastic tees or tees with a glossy finish. The glossy finish will not stick in the T-nut holes.

Roll the paint/sand texture on starting at the top of the wall and working down. Do about a 4 x 4-foot section at a time. Go over the texture up and down, then left and right.

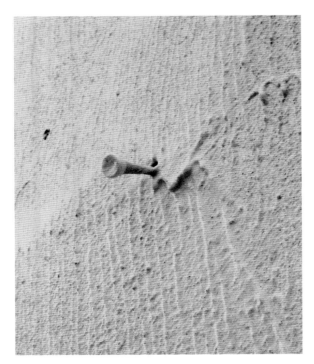

Once in a while one of the tees will pop out. Stop and replace the tee immediately. It costs less time to stop and fix the tee than it does to get the paint/sand texture out of the T-nut threads.

To make a patterned texture, use an old sock or rag. While the texture is still wet, make patterns. Swirls and wavy patterns look good and provide an evenly contoured surface for just a little footwork traction. After working with the texture, you will develop a good pattern, and it will become easier to apply.

The texture needs to dry thoroughly before the final coat of paint. This may take several days and even up to a week. The outside wall described in chapter 4 was textured in the summer during warm temperatures. It took three days before it was dry enough and hard enough to put the finishing two coats of exterior latex paint over the texture.

Before applying paint, use a drywall trowel with very light pressure over the surface of the texture

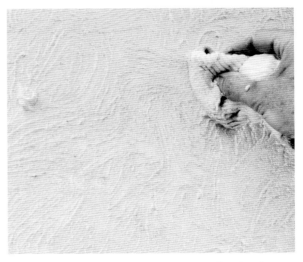

When the texture in a 4 x 4-foot section is nice and even, use a rag, old T-shirt, or sponge to create patterns in the texture.

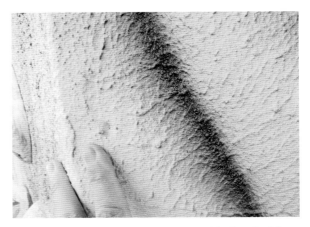

Completed homemade texture. This has held up to a variety of climbing styles, including smearing on slabs. The texture has been able to withstand normal usage.

to knock off some of the texture's peaks. Next, use a broom to whisk away any loose pieces or debris that may be clinging to the texture. Go over the entire wall, making sure you get into the crevasses and nooks created by the features.

The Bare Plywood Option

If you specifically need to practice your footwork, smearing techniques, etc., then texture will help you meet your goals. If your wall will be in a location with high humidity—for example, in a basement, or an outdoor climbing wall or garage climbing wall in a humid climate—applying a sealer and paint can extend the life of the wall.

The truth is, however, most people do not need to texture their walls. Many climbers prefer the slick plywood surface because it forces them to climb "cleanly," using only the hand and foot holds. If you live in a dry climate, you don't even need to paint or seal the bare plywood. Remember, though, that if you choose to texture your wall, then you will definitely need to seal it and paint it, even if you live in a dry climate.

APPLYING A PROTECTIVE PRIMER-SEALER COAT

Apply exterior primer-sealer in the same way that you applied the texture: vertical strokes, then horizontal strokes. This evens out the sealer across the surface. Apply the sealer in square block sections. This will allow you to get the application on in an even pattern before it starts to dry.

APPLYING EXTERIOR FINISH PAINT

After the primer-sealer has dried, apply the finish coat. The coats of primer-sealer and paint over the surface of the texture give it additional strength and protect the texture from moisture. Pick a nice color for the base coat, and get an accent color in a spray can to give the wall a design.

Installing Hand and Foot Holds

There is an extraordinary selection of climbing holds available commercially. While it is possible to make your own holds, there are so many excellent climbing-hold packages available that it is not at all necessary to put the time and cost into making your own.

You may get a better deal on holds if you buy them online. In most states you will not pay sales tax, and some vendors will ship for free if you make a purchase for a certain amount. Usually it's around $50, but it varies with the online vendor. Check out the variety from multiple vendors at indoorclimbing.com/climbingholds.

Climbing holds are easy to install. First, select the right size bolt. The length of the hole through the hold varies from hold to hold. The bolt should extend about ¼ inch through the T nut when tightened. Slip the bolt into the hold and contact the threads of the T nut. Turn it clockwise with your fingers to catch the threads. If manufacturer's instructions are not available, the bolt should be tightened about a half turn past the point where it initially becomes tight. Wiggle or shake the hold to see if there is still flex or play. If necessary, tighten in quarter turns until the hold is secure. Do not over-tighten the bolt. Overtightening may cause the hold to break.

A good assortment of climbing holds will give you versatility in setting routes.

Thread the bolt through the hold and into the T nut. Tighten a half turn past snug.

Step 6:
Addressing Fall-Zone, Maintenance, and Safety Considerations

Your work isn't over when construction is finished. You will need to make sure your climbing wall is maintained correctly and adequate padding material is installed throughout the fall zone. Set up your own house rules to make sure the wall is always used in a safe manner.

Fall Zones

Make sure you have sufficient area for the fall zone. According to the US Consumer Product Safety Commission (CPSC), "Stationary climbing equipment . . . should have a [fall] zone extending a minimum of 6 feet in all directions from the perimeter of the equipment." Do not climb above concrete, asphalt, wood, carpet, or any other hard surfaces. Be aware that falls directly onto an unprotected surface can result in serious head injury and death. Even grass and turf will lose its ability to absorb the shock of a fall through wear and weather. The fall zone must be completely clear of equipment and other obstacles.

The CPSC reports that 51,000 injuries a year happen on home playground equipment. Unfortunately, about fifteen children die each year from falls from playground equipment. A climbing wall presents a greater potential for falls due to vertical and overhung faces and the challenging nature of the routes; therefore, an adequate fall zone is of utmost importance for the climber's safety!

There is very little specific guidance for the thickness and type of padding for placing below home climbing walls. The table below correlates the fall height with the type and depth of padding. It was taken from the CPSC. More information can be found at cpsc.gov/cpscpub/pubs/323.html. This applies to playground climbers, but the information is applicable to home climbing gyms as well.

For indoor walls, bark and sand are very undesirable. The dust will track around the house, bark will be a haven for critters, and sand will be a tempting potty stop for the family cat. However, for an outdoor wall these materials work pretty well when used with a commercial crash pad.

Some commercial climbing gyms use shredded rubber in their fall zone. Shredded rubber, also called rubber mulch, is made from recycled tires. Shredded rubber works well for both indoor and outdoor climbing walls. Almost all tires have steel wire and polyester fibers running through the rubber for strength. When recycled for use in playgrounds, the recycling process completely removes the wire and polyester fibers. Shredded rubber should be installed 6 to 9 inches thick throughout the fall zone. Be sure to research your specific fall-zone material depth requirements on the cpsc.gov website. Rubber mulch has advantages over wood bark or sand because it is relatively clean, bugs don't seem to like it, it drains water and holds up

Type and Amount of Material and Fall-Zone Depth

Type of Material	6-inch Depth	9-inch Depth	12-inch Depth
Double-shredded bark mulch	6 feet	10 feet	11 feet
Wood chips	7 feet	10 feet	11 feet
Fine sand	5 feet	5 feet	9 feet
Fine gravel	6 feet	7 feet	10 feet

to weather, and it does not track dirt if used inside. If you decide to price rubber mulch, be sure to specify that you want the playground grade. Other grades are less expensive, but they are not as clean or may not have the steel wire and fibers removed.

CLEARANCE AROUND THE CLIMBING WALL

The CPSC has produced a document called "Home Playground Safety Tips." While it is not specifically written for home climbing walls, the principles and recommendations are good to consider. It recommends the clear zone (use zone) should extend 6 feet from the farthest extruding point, and protective surfacing material should be placed throughout this area. The key is to allow enough room for the climber to swing, or miss a dyno. Both climber and spotter need to land in the fall zone without danger of striking an object or wall. Keep the fall zone clear of equipment or other obstacles except, of course, the spotter and maybe a bag of chalk.

Maintenance

Keep your climbing wall in top shape with regular maintenance. Over time, holds will loosen, wood will splinter, or texture may need repair. Be observant, and monitor the wall at all times. The most common maintenance item is replacing a spinning T nut. The process below explains an effective method for fixing a spinner.

HOW TO REPLACE A SPINNING T NUT

You need access to the back side of your climbing wall to repair a spinning T nut. Without a reference of some kind, it will be difficult to locate the spinner, so before you climb behind the wall, stick something through the hole of the spinning T nut. Make sure it is long enough to protrude through the T nut to the back. Once you are behind the wall, you will be able to quickly locate it among the other T nuts.

T nuts will spin for various reasons. The most likely reason for spinning is that the teeth on the

To locate the spinning T nut on the back side of the wall, stick something through the hole. This will help you find it among the sea of T nuts.

Press the T nut into the hole. Only use light tapping with a hammer, just enough force to hold it in place. If you are working with a partner, he can thread a bolt through a hold into the T nut as you hold it from the back side.

T nut have bent. Put some wood glue in the hole, then put the T nut back in the hole. Press it in as far as possible by hand. Using a wood block, you can press against the T nut and tap the wood block with moderate force. Hammering too hard will weaken the screws holding the plywood in place. The idea is just to get the T nut in place, not deeply seated. When it's in place, go around to the front of the wall and use a large climbing hold to screw it in, tightening and pulling the T nut into the hole. Pull it in tightly, then remove the hold and leave the T nut alone for a few hours while the wood glue dries.

Sometimes the T-nut hole becomes too enlarged to seat a T nut. The best thing to do in this case is just abandon it and drill another hole and mount a new T nut using the process described above.

Safety Considerations

Climbing on artificial walls has risks. Minimize risks with good judgment, careful planning, and preparation. The following safety tips are not comprehensive. In fact, it's not possible to cover every situation. Your safety is your responsibility. Keep the following tips in mind for creating a safe environment in your specific climbing wall area.

CONDUCT A PRE-CLIMBING INSPECTION

Before climbing, conduct a safety inspection of the wall. Overtightening holds can cause stress cracks and may cause the hold to break. Check for cracks around the bolt holes. If you find a cracked hold, remove and replace it.

Look behind the wall at the structural support system. Structural weakening and possible failure of key support members may occur if water is allowed to soak into the climbing wall. Rot can weaken previously solid wood to the point of failure. Look for signs of rot, weakened joints, fatigue in the metal joints, tightness of the joints, and the like. Rot is caused by a fungus. As the fungus grows, it changes the color of the wood. Inspect the wood for rot or signs of rot by examining it for yellowish or brown discoloration. The chance of wood rot can be mitigated by keeping your climbing wall dry and ventilated.

CONTROLLING ACCESS

For outdoor climbing walls, check local ordinances about the need for a fence. Some towns require fencing for playground climbers, and the same would apply to an outdoor climbing wall. For indoor walls you may be able to lock the door to control access. If there is no lock on the door, consider installing one.

INSURANCE

You may need or want additional insurance coverage to protect yourself in case a guest gets hurt. Ask your insurance agent.

RULES

Make some ground rules for children and adult guests to follow such as the age for unsupervised climbing, climbing in pairs, height limits, jumping, etc. Implement rules that make the most sense for your situation.

Here are some suggestions. Use them as ideas for developing your own site-specific safety rules for your climbing wall.

- Stretch for 15 minutes prior to climbing.
- Always make sure your crash pads, mats, and landing surfaces are in place, with no gaps exposing the floor.
- Climb with a spotter; avoid climbing alone.
- Do not climb over or under another climber.
- Remove jewelry, bracelets, watches, and any bulky items from pockets before climbing. Items such as these can cause injury if you land on them, and they could tear the crash pad.
- Experienced climbers should help beginners with tips and safety.
- Minors should not be unsupervised. There must be at least one person over the age of 18.

SPOTTING

Climbing with someone else is more fun than climbing alone. When you have a partner, each of you gets a chance to rest in between sets. You and your partner can take turns on a problem and offer each other "beta"—tips and hints. Besides the training value you get from each other, a spotter is a key link in bouldering safety.

A spotter's job is to guide the fall, not catch the fall. Good spotters develop their own technique and skill. Pay particular attention to protecting the climber's head from hitting anything. Spotters give the climber a little extra confidence, and sometimes a little assistance will help the climber complete a sequence. The spotter should lightly touch the back and waist of the climber. A light, sensitive contact touching the waist or hips will not change the climber's balance and will give the spotter added sensory cues when the climber is about to peel.

CHAPTER 3

Using Your Climbing Wall

You'll be anxious to get started climbing on your new wall. Your skills will improve quickly, so now is the time to upgrade to new climbing gear, learn some fun and social climbing games, and improve your route-setting skills.

The Gear You Need

The great thing about having your own climbing wall is the freedom and quick access you will have. After you fit your wall with climbing holds, all you'll need are some good bouldering shoes, a chalk bag, and a crash pad, and you're ready to go.

Climbing Shoes

Slip-on climbing—or bouldering—shoes are designed for easy on-off. If you want maximum performance from your bouldering shoes, you

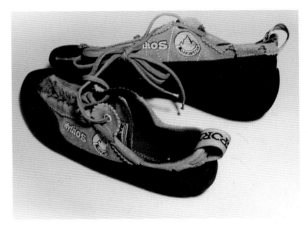

Climbing shoes are an essential gear item.

will want a tight fit. To get this, you will sacrifice a little comfort. For this reason boulderers tend to prefer either the slip closure or the hook-and-loop closure. A highly downturned toe will give you an advantage when hooking into small jibs and pockets. The midsole is more flexible than a sport climbing shoe, and the rubber isn't as thick. Each brand sizes differently, so the best thing to do is try them on before buying.

Get Gear Here

You can find all the climbing gear you need at indoorclimbing.com/gear.

You're done with construction . . . now it's time to start using your wall!

Chalk Bag

Bouldering routes require the best possible grip and friction, as do highly technical sport routes. Bouldering is unique in that the routes are shorter and typically more technically difficult. Due to this difference, a boulderer may not need to "chalk up" while on the wall. Community chalk bags are made just for this kind of climbing. Community bags are placed on the floor and allow groups to take turns on the wall, chalking up before getting on the route. Another option, shown in the photo, is the individually worn chalk bags. They attach with a string or belt with a clip closure. You can also get chalk balls to keep your hands dry. They are usually placed inside a chalk bag, but they can also be set on a nearby table if you don't want to wear the chalk bag while climbing. The final option for keeping your hands dry is liquid chalk, which is a liquid magnesium solution. It effectively increases friction between your hands and the holds, and there is no dust.

Exercise, stress, and excitement will make the palms of your hands sweat. The sweat makes your grip slippery. Chalk absorbs the moisture and improves your grip.

Climbing games are an effective way to train while having fun as a group.
©JAN KRANENDONK / LICENSED BY SHUTTERSTOCK.COM

Crash Pads

When you fall from a bouldering problem, you will want some thick padding to help break your fall. A crash pad has a layered foam interior encased in a nylon cover. The upper layer is usually about 4 centimeters thick and functions to distribute the force of impact into the pad. The lower layer of foam is softer and conforms to the shape of the surface below it. Bouldering pads provide excellent protection, and when used with a spotter, they significantly reduce the potential for injury.

Cleaning Brush

A cleaning brush is used to break the grime and grease out of the pores of the hold material. With a lot of use, the holds become slippery. Oils from your skin and sweat from the palms of your hands seep into the holds and make it more difficult to get a good grip. Some climbers put a toothbrush in the loop of their chalk bag. The toothbrush is lightweight, does not interfere, and can be easily accessed while climbing to quickly clean a grimy hold. Any small stiff-bristle brush will work fine.

A standard stiff-bristle cleaning brush is useful for keeping your holds clean. As you climb, the sweat and oils from your hands build up in the tiny pockets on the surface of the holds. When this happens, the holds become slippery. Just rub the bristles directly on the holds.

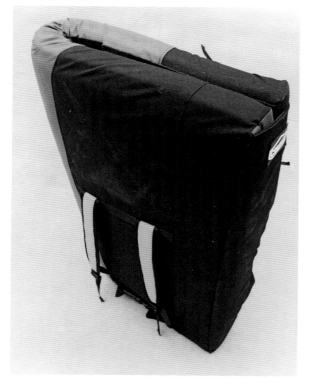

Crash pads are specially designed for bouldering. When used with a spotter, climbers will greatly reduce their risk of injury.

Climbing Games

There are many climbing games you can play with friends and climbing partners. It's easier to keep pushing yourself when you are having fun, and climbing is definitely a social activity. Climbing games will create an enjoyable atmosphere and offer excellent training value at the same time. Here are some of the most popular climbing games.

Add-on

Start Add-on with a two- or three-move sequence. The first climber traverses the sequence, then reaches out with either a foot or hand and marks the next hold location. The second climber gets on the same route and completes the sequence, including the new hold, then marks one additional hand or foot hold. If the wall already has holds, simply mark the next hold with a piece of chalk. It's interesting to strip the wall and play this game by adding new hand and foot holds as you go. Add-on can also be played with hands only. In this variation, usually the wall has a full set of hand and foot holds. The climber marks only handholds, and any foothold is "on route." Repeat this pattern until one of the climbers cannot complete the sequence, or until both are exhausted. This will help develop endurance and teach you how to preview a route.

Pointer

This game is played with a climber and a pointer. The person on the ground points to the next hold while the climber is making the previous move. You can play this game by waiting for completion of the move, then pointing, but it makes the game more static. It helps the climber to look ahead to the next move and use momentum and flow while finishing the current move. The person on the ground should learn to anticipate the climber's movement, and point out routes at the top of the climber's level. This is an excellent climber/trainer routine. However, it can also be played as a competition between two equally matched climbers. In this variation,

if a climber cannot make a move, the pointer will get on the route and attempt the move he just set for the climber. If he can do it, he gets a point. The new climber and pointer continue until a move cannot be done, and then they switch again.

Memory

This is a valuable game for competition climbers. Before they begin, the climbers preview their route. Then they have to return to the isolation area. Competition climbers need to remember the route and sequences they observed during the preview. This game will help develop sequence memory and improve on-sight competition climbing. In training it is played by a climber and coach or a buddy. The person on the ground points out a few moves to get started. The climber then climbs the route, remembering each hold in the sequence and using each of them. The climber hops down when finished, and the trainer points out another set.

Take-Away

In this game two climbers of approximately equal ability make a traverse route with plenty of holds. The route is marked with chalk. After each climber finishes the traverse, he picks a hold and rubs off a mark, eliminating the hold from the route. If the next climber is unable to complete the traverse, the person who removed the hold is challenged to complete the traverse. If he cannot do it, the mark is put back on, but if he can, he wins the game. A variation on this game is played with many climbers. Each climber takes turns climbing the route, cycling back to the original climber who took the last hold off the route. If everyone is able to complete the traverse, the next climber in the sequence takes off a mark, removing another hold from the route. The cycle continues through the group so that everyone gets a chance to take off a hold. When someone cannot complete the traverse, he is eliminated. The remaining climbers continue. The last climber able to complete the route is the winner.

Route Setting

Route setting can be a workout in itself, as well as an engaging mental challenge. With a home climbing wall, you have a unique opportunity to focus your training in very specific ways. You can work training routines into your workouts to give yourself exactly what you need, when you need it. On top of the improvements you will notice in your climbing ability, route setting is fun and gives a real sense of satisfaction . . . and you may find your routes are never truly done. That's the best way to hone your route-setting skills: Keep experimenting, trying, testing. Here are a few route-setting principles that will help you set good training routes.

It starts with a concept: for example, to improve upper body strength, or to improve balance and footwork and the like. Choose the type of holds that match the type of climbing, and lay them out on the floor in front of the wall in the rough order of use. Referring back to the example, upper body strength requires solid, positive holds, whereas balance and footwork require small holds. When you lay them out, check them for wear, cracks, and chips. Place bolts in the bolt holes. Make sure the bolt extends at least an inch past the back of the hold. (Remember that this distance is necessary to go through the ¾-inch plywood with ¼ inch left over to allow for texture.)

Looking at the wall, visualize the holds and mark some locations with chalk or tape. Start with the big picture and establish the concept. Don't let yourself spend too much time with specific sequences. Just get the basic path and feel laid out. Next, place climbing holds at the chalk- or tape-marked locations. Set the handholds first, then the footholds. Climb your route from bottom to top—then the tweaking begins. A ladder will help you save energy. Step onto the route from the ladder when working out a sequence. Tweak the angles and positions, and even replace the holds with different-size holds.

Colored Tape

Rather than rely on colored holds to mark a route, mark all the holds of a particular route in one color using colored tape stuck next to the hold. This way you can have multiple overlapping routes on your climbing wall. You can get colored tape at just about any craft store, department store, or hardware store. Use any tape that's easy to see—black electrical tape, blue painter's tape, masking tape, or the like.

Here are some things to keep in mind while route setting:

- Focus on a consistent level of difficulty. An entire route will seem more difficult than each individual section.

- If you have a crux, try to keep it a half grade more difficult than the overall grade of the route. Don't locate a crux at the start or finish. Let the climber make a few moves before and after the crux.

- Think about falling from each hold. Is it safe? Set routes that allow a climber to fall safely.

- Create variety and interest by using different types of holds, varying the direction, and using features if you have them.

Colored tape works great for route setting.
© PLUS 69/SHUTTERSTOCK.COM

Route setting can be captivating . . . you'll want to design the perfect route.
© ALYSTA/LICENSED BY SHUTTERSTOCK.COM

- Avoid setting reachy routes. Newbies tend to try to create difficulty by spacing the holds farther apart. You will grow faster as a route setter if you keep this in mind.

Route Setting to Achieve a Performance Goal

You can set routes to target the type of climbing you want to improve. For example, bouldering requires strength and dynamic movements. Face climbing requires endurance. Sport climbing and indoor climbing combine strength and endurance. Here are some techniques that can be used when setting routes to achieve a specific performance goal:

- Teaching the climber to read a route in advance. Start in the middle of the route. Set a move combination that can only be done if started with a particular hand (left or right). From an incorrect hand position, set holds backward in a logical sequence of left, right, left, etc., to the start position. If the climber does not read the route before beginning, he will arrive at the sequence with hands reversed. If he reads the

route before starting, he will climb with hands reversed through the lower, easier moves to the sequence and be able to do the move with hands in the correct position. This will teach climbers to read the route before starting.

- Improving balance and smoothness while climbing. Add a slab with a positive angle (not overhanging) of 60 degrees or greater. Set only footholds, making the route a feet-only traverse. The climber can use hands for balance only. Set a high and low traverse back and forth. This simple exercise will help beginning climbers develop their sense of balance.

- Keeping the body close to the wall. If hand and foot holds are far enough apart, a climber can stand relatively erect. Many novice climbers let their butts and bodies hang out away from the wall. A setting technique to teach climbers to keep their body weight close to the wall is to place the hand and foot holds close vertically. If the climber doesn't do a kneedrop or some other maneuver to keep body weight in, the knees will force the butt and body to hang out too far. Small holds will make it impossible to stay on the wall when body weight is pulling the climber out. If the body is close to the wall, the force pulling out will not be as great, and they will be able to stick the hold.

- Learning to dead-point. This is an important basic movement to master. The dead point is the exact top of an arc where the body changes direction from up to down, and is the point where a new hold is grasped. To practice this movement, set holds just beyond the fingertips. This will require climbers to extend the body position and smoothly grasp the next hold at the dead point. As they improve, the distance can be extended.

- Gaining endurance. To help gain endurance, smoothness, and a consistent speed of climbing, you can set an easy route or circuit with no cruxes. A good pattern is a circle or figure eight

Route Setting with a Partner

It's good to work with someone else when setting routes. Two route setters can help prevent each other from getting stale, or in other words, from always setting similar problems and in a similar style. Two people working together will come up with a creative set of sequences that neither of them would have done if working alone. Also, you need a spotter. You can take turns on sections. The spotter has a different vantage than the climber, in that he can see the whole route, not just the sequence.

on the wall. Climb while being conscious of your body movements. Listen to the sound of your feet. If you can hear them slapping and scraping, try to consciously place your feet on a hold without any sound. Strive to climb relaxed, smoothly, and deliberately throughout the circuit, repeating it many times consecutively.

- Learning how to use rest spots. Learning to recognize when to rest and what to rest on is a key skill for climbers. To help develop this skill, build in a rest spot before a series of difficult power moves. As a route setter of your home climbing wall, you can create these rest spots with larger holds. A protruding hold that is big enough for a knee to wedge under might make a good rest spot. A rest spot may simply be a knob that you put your shoulder against. Creating rest locations in your route also helps you recognize rest opportunities and use this technique when you are climbing at other locations.

- Practicing specific types of moves. You can set routes that require a specific type of move, like the kneedrop, high step, figure four, heel hook, etc. Get your friends on the route and observe without telling them what you intended. See if they use the technique you intended or if they come up with another solution to get past the crux. It takes a little practice to set a route that can only be done one way.

- Setting routes for fun. These types of routes are creative by design but not particularly difficult or cruxy. Often you can just set something easy and have some buddies over to play a game of Take-away or Add-on and come up with some very fun and creative routes. This is really the key: Have fun. If you enjoy what you are doing, you will improve in leaps and bounds!

One of the best things to do is observe other route setters when you go to the gym. Talk about route setting with other climbers. Think about the value of a route from a training perspective when you climb in your local gym, and then think about setting a similar type of route at your home gym.

Climbing Wall Examples

This chapter provides examples of climbing walls from concept to completion. The examples demonstrate the process described in chapter 2, Building a Climbing Wall Step-by-Step. In this chapter there is an example of an inexpensive small garage climbing wall, which might be a good starter wall for climbers on a budget. The next example shows how to convert the small garage wall to incorporate a panel with an adjustable angle, enhancing the training value of a small wall. The final example is a seven-sided outdoor climbing wall suitable for all ages and climber skill levels.

Building a Small Garage Climbing Wall

Using the six steps below will benefit you even for small climbing walls such as this example.

Step 1: Planning and Designing Your Wall

In this step we develop the concept and establish the conditions and constraints. For this example the location is chosen in a small available space on one wall in a garage. Space and budget are limited.

There is only room for two panels, and the budget will be around $100. The training goal is to improve endurance and simply provide a workout area through the winter. The wall for this training goal should be vertical or slightly overhung, not more than 10 degrees. This will allow for a continuous circuit route for endurance and stamina training.

Step 2: Making a Sketch and a Model

The sketch is the next natural step after planning. The conditions have been established, so the sketch is the illustration of the wall that meets the conditions. Of course, you can make more than one sketch. There could be many shapes that meet your conditions. In this example space and budget influence the size and shape.

Step 3: Gathering Materials and Tools

Develop the materials list from the sketch and model. Look at each section, each joint, each piece, and write down the materials they require. To develop a tool list, look at each material piece and note which tools are needed to make or install it.

If budget is a concern, just get started with an inexpensive two panel 8' x 8' climbing wall. You will get a lot of training value for the cost, and you can always expand later.

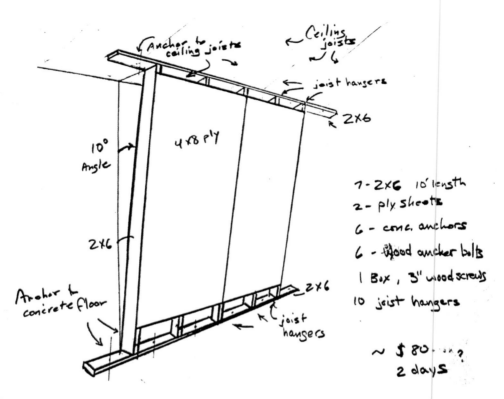

Anchor to
ceiling joists

Ceiling
joists

joist hangers

2X6

10°
Angle

4 x 8 ply

2X6

7 - 2X6 10' length
2 - ply sheets
6 - conc. anchors
6 - wood anchor bolts
1 Box , 3" wood screws
10 joist hangers

~ $80...?
2 days

Anchor to
concrete floor

2X6

joist
hangers

A sketch of a simple garage climbing wall that meets your training objectives and budget sets you up for the next steps of gathering tools and quantifying materials.

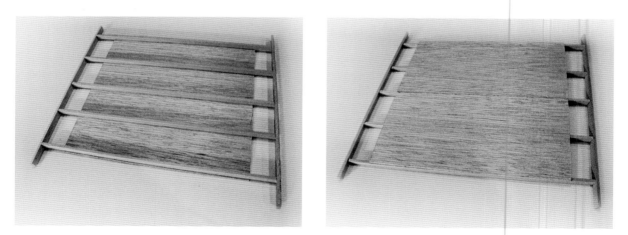

The model helps you visualize the project in three dimensions and formulate the sequence of construction.

Materials List

Description	Quantity	Source *Store A*	Item Total	Source *Store B*	Item Total
Wood glue	1	$5.00	$5.00	$4.50	**$4.50**
2" wood screws	1	$4.50	$4.50	$4.00	**$4.00**
3" wood screws	1	$5.00	**$5.00**	$5.50	$5.50
3/4" plywood	2	$18.00	**$36.00**	$20.00	$40.00
Concrete anchors	6	$2.00	**$12.00**	$2.00	$12.00
Wood anchors	6	$1.00	**$6.00**	$1.00	$6.00
2 x 6 x 10 lumber	7	$6.50	**$45.50**	$6.30	**$44.10**
Joist hangers	10	$0.90	**$9.00**	$1.10	$11.00
			$123.00		**$127.10**

Lowest Total: $120.60

The materials were roughly estimated on the drawing. The more detailed list turned out to be more expensive. A cost comparison was done, but it only saved a few dollars. However, on larger projects cost comparisons may save hundreds of dollars.

Tool List

Circular saw

Drill with Phillips bit attachment

4-foot level

Chalk line

Tape measure

Framer's pencils

Extension cords

Gloves, safety goggles, earplugs

Framing square

Stepladder

Work bench

C clamps and wood clamps

Hammer

Tool belt

String

Laser level

Stud finder

Circular sander drill attachment

Angle finder

T bevel

The tool list is developed at the same time as the materials list. Consider each item in the materials list and think about the tools you'll need for the task or tasks for which the materials are to be used.

Step 4: Constructing Your Climbing Wall

With the materials, tools, and plans in place, we can begin construction. The first step is to anchor the top and bottom plates. This climbing wall extends in a continuous wall from the floor to the ceiling. This is the simplest method of construction.

After drilling the pilot holes, lag screws secure the top plate to the ceiling joists.

According to the Rise-Run Chart in appendix D, for a desired angle of 10 degrees with a wall height of 9 feet, the distance between the top plate and the wall should be 19 inches. Pilot holes will be drilled through the top plate into the ceiling joists. The pilot hole should be the size of the shaft of the lag screw, smaller than the diameter of the threads.

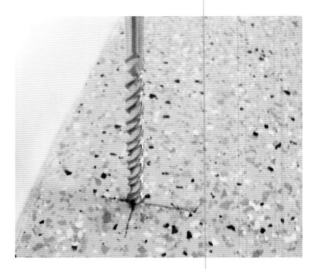

The bottom plate is anchored to the concrete floor using concrete expanding anchors. A hole is drilled in the bottom plate using a wood screw. A pilot hole is drilled in the concrete using a concrete screw. The pilot hole is drilled about ½ inch deeper than the depth of the anchor.

The expanding concrete anchor is set in place with a hammer.

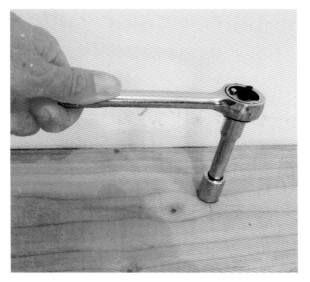

Once set, the bolt is turned and the anchor engages and expands. This provides a secure anchor in concrete.

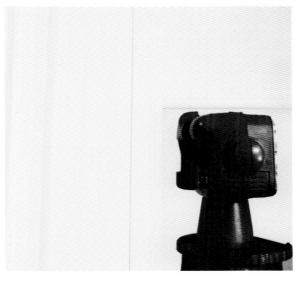

With the top and bottom plates in place, the locations of the studs must be set. Vertical plumb is established from the top plate and projected down to the bottom plate using a laser level.

The laser level projects the location of the center of the stud from the top plate. The stud location is marked.

The angle of the wall will be 10 degrees. A string is fastened to the top and bottom plates at the location where the studs will be placed. Using the string, the left-right plumb is checked, and the 10-degree angle is checked with an angle finder.

A T bevel is used to copy and transfer the angle for marking on other pieces. In this case the angle is known to be exactly 10 degrees. However, in some cases the angle may not be known in advance. Use a T bevel to transfer an angle for marking. Use an angle finder to determine the numeric value of the angle.

The stud is marked using the angle transferred by the T bevel. The stud will be held in place with a joist hanger. The stud should be cut so it fits squarely into the heel of the joist hanger.

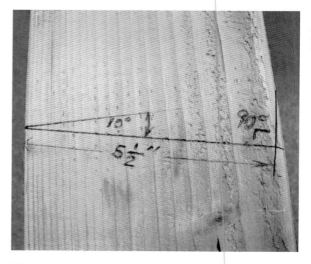

The studs attach to the plates, which are 5½ inches wide. Therefore, the heel of the stud should be cut at 90 degrees at the 5½-inch mark.

This is how the stud should be cut to fit the joist hanger.

All studs are initially secured in place with one or two small nails. If small adjustments are necessary, they can be done at this time.

The stud is screwed into place, meeting the 5½-inch top plate with no part of the stud overhanging.

Once the studs are perfectly aligned, slip the joist hangers in place for the top and bottom joints of all studs.

Joist hangers are screwed into place, securing the studs to the top and bottom plates.

Construction is complete after just one evening's work.

You will need someone to help hold the plywood in place as you attach the screws. Before lifting the plywood sheet in place, start some screws. This will make it much easier to attach the sheet while holding it in place.

Step 5: Adding Features, Texture, and Holds

No texture or features need to be added to this climbing wall. The climbing holds are a mixture of commercial and homemade screw-ons. Since budget was a concern on this project, cost savings were realized by eliminating the need for T nuts and by making half of the holds from scrap lumber.

Work with the sander until you get the shape you like.

Using scraps from the construction, roughly cut random shapes. Large shapes are less likely to break than small shapes.

Using a circular sander drill attachment, sand the rough edges.

Drill two pilot holes per wooden hold. Countersink each pilot hole so the head of the screw sinks below the surface of the hold.

It took 3 hours to make this small assortment of wooden holds.

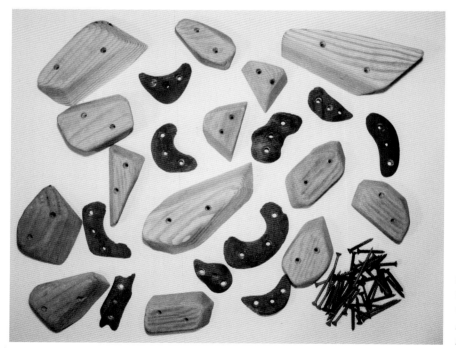

The full set of holds for this climbing wall were the fourteen homemade wooden holds and a Metolius ten-pack of screw-on climbing holds.

Do not overtighten screw-on climbing holds. Wooden climbing holds will split if the screw is driven too deeply into the hold. Commercial screw-on holds may crack or break if overtightened.

Step 6: Addressing Fall-Zone, Maintenance, and Safety Considerations

The fall zone is clear of obstructions and the crash pad fits easily underneath the climbing wall. All joints are easy to access for visual inspection and maintenance.

This design provides easy access to all joints and anchors for visual inspection and maintenance.

With a fall zone in place, it's time to climb. A two-panel wall is the minimum size to build. One panel would be about the same size as a large campus board.

Even a small two-panel wall will greatly enhance your training opportunities. Nothing beats the convenience and immediate access of your own climbing wall, even if it's small.

Building an Adjustable-Angle Climbing Wall

This is an example of expanding the functionality of an existing wall. The conditions remain the same, but the training goals have expanded to include strength training.

Step 1: Planning and Designing Your Wall

Strength training is accomplished by short sequences of high intensity and power. A steeper overhang is needed for this training goal. However, with space limited, adding another panel is not an option. Therefore, we will maximize use of this small area by modifying a two-panel wall to have an adjustable angle. This will offer the ability to do both strength training at a steeper overhang, and technical and endurance training using the more vertical angles.

Step 2: Making a Sketch and a Model

The two-panel wall is modified so one panel pivots on a lag bolt, and both the top and bottom are secured.

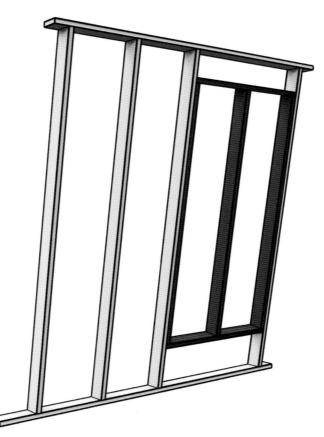

This sketch was modified from the two-panel garage climbing wall. Google Sketchup was used to create this sketch. The red colored framework highlights the changes necessary to convert the fixed climbing wall to an adjustable climbing wall.

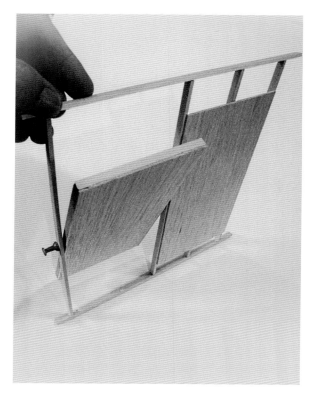

The model of the garage climbing wall was modified according to the drawing.

This is the view of the back side of the garage climbing wall model.

Step 3: Gathering Materials and Tools

This example is adapted from the garage climbing wall described earlier. Therefore, the materials and tools are the same.

Step 4: Constructing Your Climbing Wall

Since this is a modification of an existing climbing wall, the wall is disassembled, modified, and then rebuilt according to the modified sketch and model.

The first step is to remove the center stud, opening a space for the adjustable section.

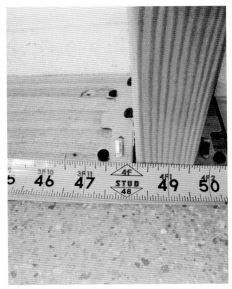

The outer stud needs to move out by 1½ inches to fit the adjustable 4-foot-wide plywood panel.

Assemble the adjustable section on the floor.

Tack the joints together with a small nail. This step is to hold the frame in place while you square it.

A squared frame has equal diagonals. Measure each diagonal. Compare the distances. The greater diagonal distance needs to have its corner pushed in, the lesser, pulled out. Remeasure both and continue repeating this process until both diagonals are equal.

When the frame is square, the joints are secured with 3-inch wood screws.

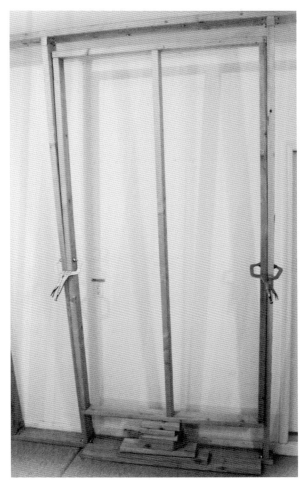

Clamp the frame in place.

Drill holes for the hex bolts. The frame will pivot on the bolt while adjusting the angle.

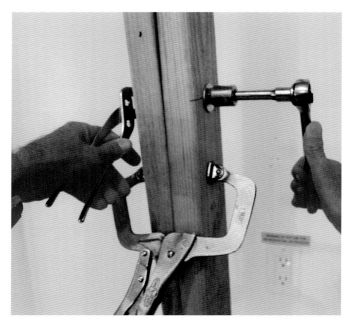

Insert a washer on both sides of the hex bolt and tighten.

The adjustable frame section is in place prior to securing the four corners.

Thick-gauge tie straps are used to hold the four corners at the desired angle.

Top corners held firmly in place as viewed from the outside.

Step 5: Adding Features, Texture, and Holds

Since this is a modification of the first example, this step has already been completed.

Step 6: Addressing Fall-Zone, Maintenance, and Safety Considerations

The fall zone is the same as the garage climbing wall. The attach points on the adjustable wall should be inspected carefully.

Additionally, a safety strap is added. In the unlikely event that every attach point fails, this strap will keep the adjustable section from falling.

To add the safety strap, an eye bolt is screwed into the back of the adjustable panel and another into the ceiling joist. Pilot holes are drilled for installation of the eye bolt.

Eye bolts were placed into a ceiling joist and the adjustable panel. In the photo, webbing was clipped to the eye bolts using locking carabiners. Note that safety straps purchased from your local hardware store may be cheaper than two locking carabiners.

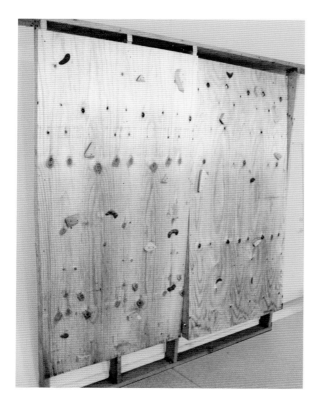

The completed adjustable climbing wall with the adjustable section is set to vertical.

Here the adjustable section has been tilted to 20 degrees.

Building an Outdoor Climbing Wall

An outdoor climbing wall poses additional challenges to the builder. Protection from the elements is a prime concern. Exposed wood must be sealed or protected from moisture. This can be done in one of two ways: Either use pressure-treated wood or prime all exposed wood with a primer-sealer.

Some sources only recommend using pressure-treated wood for outside climbing walls. I say, yes and no. If you want to texture your wall, it may be better not to use pressure-treated wood. A small, inexpensive, untextured or unpainted outdoor

climbing wall would be a good project for using pressure-treated lumber. But even pressure-treated lumber will crack with exposure to the sun and moisture.

However, if you want to paint or texture your wall, it is not necessary to use treated wood. The key is to keep moisture away from the wood.

Step 1: Planning and Designing Your Wall

For this climbing wall, the objectives are having fun and socializing, with mixed difficulty for adults and an easy incline for beginners. The idea is to make a

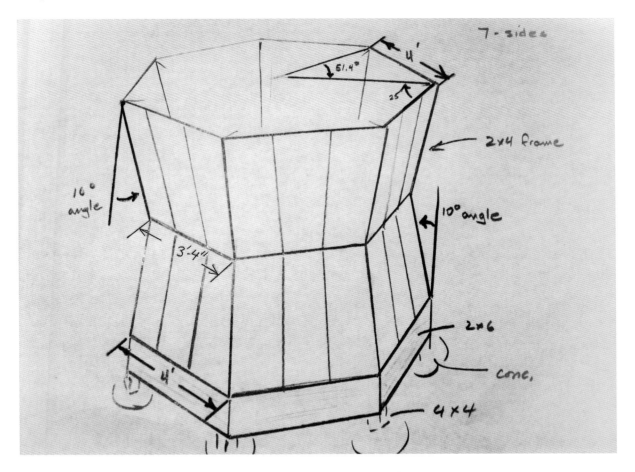

Sketch of the outdoor climbing wall. This is a seven-sided climbing structure.

framework that can be anchored into the ground. The lower section will be positively inclined, while the top will have a negative inclination. The circular shape will give it stability and enclose the back side of the wall for protection from the elements. The lower inward-leaning section will be fun for children and won't extend too high for them. The higher section will lean outward for more advanced climbers. Primer, paint, and texture will be used for both protection from the outdoor environment and for creating a surface for smearing on the lower positive incline.

Step 2: Making a Sketch and a Model

When the sketch is made, we can visualize the concept. Features will be added to help make it look interesting, and a decorative accent design will be painted over the finish coat.

Step 3: Gathering Materials and Tools

After the sketch and model are completed, the materials are estimated and the required tools are listed.

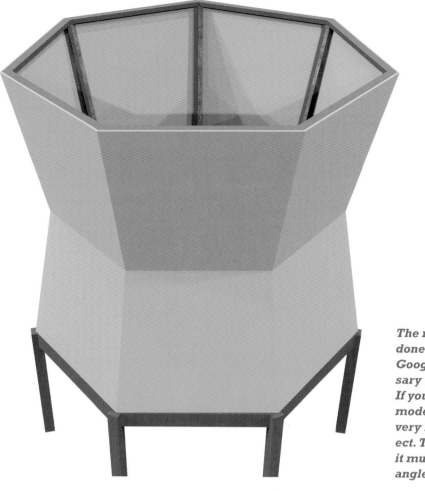

The model for this project was done with a computer using Google SketchUp. It's not necessary to make a physical model. If you know how to use CAD or modeling software, it will be very helpful throughout the project. The computer model makes it much easier to determine the angles and measurements.

Materials List

Description	Quantity	Source **Store A**	Item Total	Source **Store B**	Item Total
Roller cover	2	$4.00	$8.00	$3.00	**$6.00**
Stir stick	1	$0.30	$0.30	$0.25	**$0.25**
Primer-sealer	2	$11.00	**$22.00**	$12.00	$24.00
Screws - box 2"	1	$4.50	**$4.50**	$5.00	$5.00
Golf tees (bag)	3	$4.00	$12.00	$3.50	**$10.50**
Bulch - bags	34	$3.50	**$119.00**	$4.50	$153.00
Joint cement 5 gal	1	$20.00	$20.00	$18.00	**$18.00**
Rope	1	$5.00	$5.00	$4.50	**$4.50**
Exterior paint	2	$15.00	**$30.00**	$18.00	$36.00
Bungee bag of 4	1	$4.00	**$4.00**	$4.50	$4.50
L bracket	7	$1.20	**$8.40**	$1.30	$9.10
Wood glue	1	$5.00	$5.00	$4.50	**$4.50**
5 gal bucket	1	$5.00	$5.00	$3.00	**$3.00**
Concrete mix	7	$5.00	$35.00	$4.50	**$31.50**
Box wood screws	1	$4.50	$4.50	$4.00	**$4.00**
T-nuts bulk rate	2000	$0.20	**$400.00**	$0.30	$600.00
3/4" plywood	7	$20.00	$140.00	$18.00	**$126.00**
3" screws	1	$5.00	**$5.00**	$5.50	$5.50
Saw horse	2	$20.00	$40.00	$17.00	**$34.00**
Phillips bit for drill	2	$0.70	**$1.40**	$0.90	$1.80
3" angle brace	7	$1.00	$7.00	$0.90	**$6.30**
4x4x10' posts	4	$8.00	**$32.00**	$9.00	$36.00
2x4x96"	56	$2.20	$123.20	$1.98	**$110.88**
Play sand	1	$3.30	$3.30	$2.80	**$2.80**
Landscape fabric	3	$6.00	$18.00	$5.00	**$15.00**
Vinyl tubing per foc	8	$0.30	**$2.40**	$0.45	$3.60
Tie plates	7	$0.60	**$4.20**	$0.90	$6.30
2x6x8	7	$3.65	**$25.55**	$4.50	$31.50
Skewable angle	7	$2.35	**$16.45**	$3.40	$23.80
			$1,101.20		**$1,317.33**

Lowest Total: $1,052.13

Materials list with cost comparison between stores.

Tool List

Circular saw	Sawhorses
Chop saw or miter saw	Drop cloth, roller, roller frame, 5-gallon bucket
Drill with Phillips bit attachment	Roller screen, paintbrushes
4-foot level	C clamps and wood clamps
Chalk line	7/16" spade-type drill bit for T nuts
Tape measure	Hammer
Framer's pencils	Tool belt
Extension cords	String
Gloves, safety goggles, earplugs	Laser level
Framing square	Stud finder
Stepladder	T-bevel

With quantities determined, the supplies are purchased. Lay out the lumber in an orderly and organized way so you can find what you need quickly during the next step, construction.

The sod must be cleared before construction can be started. The fall zone consists of mulch, which will be added after the climbing wall is completed.

Step 4: Constructing Your Climbing Wall

The climbing wall is about 8 feet in diameter. Sod is removed in a radius of 10 feet from the center (4-foot radius + 6-foot fall zone). A stake marks the center. The perimeter of the fall zone is marked using a 10-foot string attached to a nail on the stake. Mark the perimeter by holding the string taut and circling the area.

Holes are dug for the support posts using the water-tube leveling method (see page 18). As the depth of each hole is measured, a mark is placed on the board at the water level in the tube. The water line shows the level relative to the water in the bucket. The depths of each hole is adjusted and measured repeatedly until all holes are of equal depth.

Posts are anchored in the holes with concrete. The posts will support the climbing wall, so they need to be exactly level and evenly spaced. Once the posts are in place, concrete is added to the hole.

The hole depth is leveled using the water-tube leveling method. The water level in the tube indicates the relative depth of the holes. Marks are made on the board to show the height (relative level) of the bottom of each hole.

One end of the tube is placed in a bucket of water, and the water is siphoned into the tube. The other end of the tube is taped to a board. The water level in the tube shows the relative difference in elevation between measurement points.

The structure sits on posts, which are anchored to the ground. This is done much the same way as someone would anchor a deck or fence post. The holes themselves need to go past the frost line for your area. Find the frost line depth for your area by searching online or calling your local building-code office.

Stack the plywood and mark the 8-inch grid on the top sheet. The easiest way to mark the grid is using a chalk line. Start the grid 4 inches from all sides, then mark every 8 inches.

Drill through all sheets of plywood at the same time. In this case there were seven sheets.

Concrete cannot be disturbed for 24 hours after being poured.

While the concrete is drying, there are many tasks that can be done. One of them is to mark and drill the T-nut holes. The T-nut holes can be done at any time prior to mounting the plywood to the frame.

Once the T-nut holes are drilled, any irregular shapes can be cut from the plywood sheets. For this project the plywood sheets are cut in a trapezoidal shape. Each trapezoid connects at a 51.4-degree angle on the horizontal plane (360/7 = 51.4). Due to the 10-degree vertical tilt, the actual angle between the two connecting trapezoidal sheets is 51.0 degrees. This is the actual dihedral angle. So each sheet should be cut at a bevel angle of 25.5 degrees. Of course, the difference between the connecting angle formed on the horizontal plane and the dihedral angle is only 0.2 degree. This minor difference is only noted to point out the fact that the bevel decreases as the vertical tilt increases. This difference becomes much more pronounced with overhangs and caves. For this project the bevel was set at 25 degrees. Higher accuracy is not possible or practical with a circular saw. See Cutting Dihedral Angles in chapter 2 for more information.

The plywood pieces are cut into a trapezoidal shape with a bevel of 25 degrees. When assembled they will form an inclined seven-sided shape.

The framework for the trapezoidal panels must also meet at 25 degrees. The 2 x 4s are beveled using a circular saw.

T nuts are installed after the plywood is cut to the correct shape but before the wall is assembled. A flat, horizontal surface is best for pounding the T nuts into the holes.

The panels are clamped together before fastening. Minor adjustments are made to positioning

The panels are mounted on a 2 x 6 base frame, which is fastened to the vertical posts anchored in the ground.

The lower section is assembled. The panels are fastened to the base and fastened to one another.

The upper section is assembled and fastened to the lower section.

The top and bottom sections are secured to each other and to the base framework.

Step 5: Adding Features, Texture, and Holds

The features are screwed onto the plywood sheathing after the sections are assembled but before the texture is applied. The features are made from leftover scraps from the construction. In this example there are about ten features of various lengths added to the climbing wall.

Features are formed using scraps from construction.

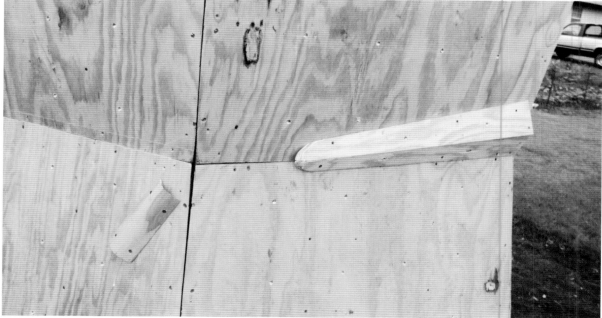

Above—Before texturing, fill small gaps at the joints using a filler. In this project expanding foam gap filler was used. This type of foam expands several times greater than its original volume and dries hard.

Left—When dry, the foam can be cut and even sanded. Excess foam is cut from the joints.

The entire climbing wall is primed and sealed.

The texture is made of a mixture of play sand, primer-sealer, and drywall topping. The drywall topping accomplishes two things: It helps suspend the sand, keeping the grains from sinking to the bottom of the bucket, and it adds body to the mixture. This texture seems to work well. When fully cured it can withstand smearing and is easy to work with in terms of application and cleanup.

After the primer-sealer is dry, the texture is applied using a roller. Golf tees are first inserted into the T nuts to protect the threads.

The texture is sealed with a primer-sealer, then the finish coat of exterior paint is applied over the entire climbing wall. The sequence of coatings should be: primer-sealer on bare wood, then texture, then primer-sealer over the texture, followed by the exterior finish paint.

Climbing holds are installed after the sealer, texture, and paint have cured. For this project we waited one full week before installing the holds.

Step 6: Addressing Fall-Zone, Maintenance, and Safety Considerations

The fall zone is a mulch. However, we will also use crash pads and proper spotting techniques. The mulch was installed at a thickness of 6 inches for 6-foot fall potential, according to the US Consumer Safety Commission's guidelines.

Because this climbing wall is located outside, it needs to be watertight. A roof must be installed and a plastic tarp will completely cover the structure. This won't seal out humidity, but it will keep direct rain and snow from accumulating and soaking into the framework. A coat of all-weather clear sealer is applied to the back side of the panel and framework.

While waiting for the texture and paint to cure, the fall zone is prepared.

The fall zone is complete by the evening of day fourteen.

Decorative paint is applied using a spray can. Holds should be installed after one week of curing the texture and paint.

The framework for the roof is constructed on a flat and level pavement surface. After assembly it is carried to the climbing wall.

The roof is lifted onto the wall and moved into place.

The roof framework is in place and ready to be fastened to the climbing wall. The framework will provide support for a plastic tarp when needed.

Angle brackets are installed to secure the roof framework.

Above—Halfway up the wall and having fun on a nice summer's day.

Right—The low sections work great for kids. The positive incline helps them stay on the wall. For more experienced climbers, the higher negative incline offers a challenging 360-degree traverse.

Trying out the lower section of the new climbing wall.

The climbing wall is wrapped up and ready for a possible rainstorm.

CHAPTER 5

Design Ideas

The purpose of this chapter is to give you ideas. These are not climbing wall designs or plans. Use these ideas in combination with one another or as an added feature in your wall, or just to spur your own creativity with a plan you are developing. Expand on these ideas or maybe develop an idea into a completely new concept. Photos start on page 109.

Design Idea #1:
Protruding Climbing Wall

This concept will maximize limited wall space. Many people need their garage for other functions besides housing a climbing wall. The studs run from the bottom plate to the top plate and are secured by joist hangers. The top and bottom plates are anchored to the ceiling joists and concrete, respectively. This idea gives you four panels, yet only takes up the wall space of one.

Design Idea #2:
Adding Large Features

Start with an easy design. Climb on it for a while, then expand. If you don't have area to expand into, you can add large features. Large features provide a challenge and fundamentally change the type of training without rebuilding or expanding. Features can be removed and reinstalled in different locations more easily than building additional wall sections.

Design Idea #3:
Low Overhang

A low overhang provides an excellent tool for strength training. If built into a corner, the sides provide support, and joists run at a 45-degree angle to the walls. There are joist hangers specifically designed to support joists at 45-degree angles.

Looking at many examples of climbing walls will help get your creative ideas flowing. Develop your unique ideas by observing and analyzing other climbing walls and adopting features that appeal to you.

Design Idea #4:
Walls with Irregular Shapes

An irregular shape is created when none of the sides are equal or parallel. In this example most of the wall is composed of irregularly shaped pieces. Not shown in the rendering are the structural connectors, such as the T brace, joist hangers, straps, and ties. Also not shown are the horizontal braces. Be sure to use metal connectors and bracing. Notice that two studs are needed to provide backing for the plywood. For measuring and cutting irregular shapes, refer to the method described under Creating Irregular Shapes in chapter 2. The miter angle of the plywood joints can be measured using a string and an angle finder. This method is described under Cutting Dihedral Angles in chapter 2. This example shows some of the possibilities you can create with irregular shapes.

Design Idea #5:
Shelf

A small shelf can easily be added to your climbing wall. Make the support for the shelf by splitting several 2 x 4s or 2 x 6s diagonally and mounting them on the existing studs. Mount a 2 x 4 or 2 x 6 flat on top of the supports to create the shelf. Cut plywood to fit. This will give you a nice feature to practice heel hooks. If placed high enough, you can also use it as a campus board, for dead hangs, dyno targets, or for pull-ups.

Design Idea #6:
Hand Jambs and Off-Width Cracks

Two 2 x 8 or 2 x 12-inch studs placed near each other will create a hand jamb or off-width crack. It is not too difficult to build a feature like this into your wall. Simply leave an opening in the plywood at the crack. The cracks do not need to be vertical, and if desired, they can even be overhanging.

Design Idea #7:
Arête and Dihedral

An arête protrudes outward into the room, and a dihedral has the opposite shape. If either the arête or dihedral is other than vertical, the angle at which the two plywood pieces meet will not equal the horizontal angle. See Cutting Dihedral Angles in chapter 2.

Design Idea #1: Protruding Climbing Wall

The framework extends beyond the climbing surface to anchor securely from the floor to the ceiling.

Design Idea #2: Adding Large Features

This three-panel climbing wall is an excellent training and workout tool.

Large features drastically change the wall, adding new and interesting challenges without increasing the area needed.

Design Idea #3: Low Overhang

This design idea makes good use of a corner space.

Four sheets of plywood provide an excellent strength-training overhang and low bouldering cave.

Design Idea #4: Walls with Irregular Shapes

This approach is different from the previous ideas in that the top and bottom plates are not the same length; however, they are parallel. This results in an irregular shape. The top and bottom plates are anchored to the ceiling joists and concrete floor, and studs connect them at the joints.

Design Idea #5: Shelf

A shelf can be added to a straight wall for practice with heel hooks.

Cracks can be simulated by placing two studs close to each other, leaving an opening. Cracks of any size and angle can easily be added to sections of your wall.

Design Idea #7: Arête and Dihedral

Dihedral and arête climbing wall.

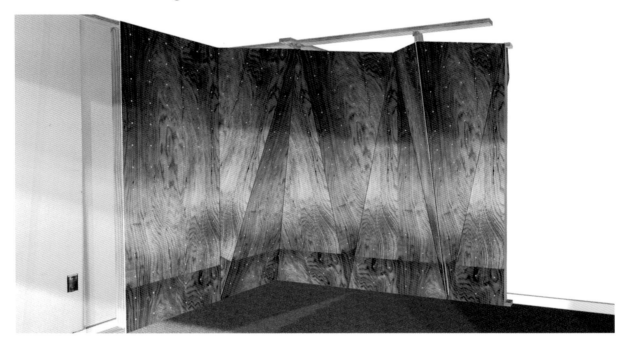

Appendix A
Frequently Asked Questions

Question: Can I use OSB or particle board? It's much less expensive.

Answer: OSB is not strong enough to use in climbing wall construction. OSB is made from wood chips pressed with glue into large sheets, then cut into a 4 x 8-foot shape. Particle board is made in a similar way with smaller particles.

Question: What size screws should I use?

Answer: For fastening structural pieces together, screws should be at least 3 inches long. This length will go through two 2 x 4s or 2 x 6s. Do not use drywall screws as they are not as strong as wood screws.

Question: How big should my climbing wall be for effective training?

Answer: It should have at least two 4 x 8-foot plywood panels. One panel would be about the same as a large campus board. However, you will not be able to traverse with one panel. Two panels will give you two or three traverse moves and give you just enough area to set up a circuit. Three panels are better, and four are better yet. Of course, the larger the climbing wall, the more expensive your project will be and the more space you will need.

Question: How much does a climbing wall cost?

Answer: The least expensive two-panel, vertical climbing wall will be about double the cost of the plywood. The garage climbing wall described earlier fits this basic profile. Get the cost of plywood, determine how many sheets you will need, and double the cost. Remember to add in additional costs for anchoring, T nuts, climbing holds, and texture or paint. Any additional design features will also push the cost up.

Question: How much floor space is needed for a climbing wall?

Answer: The minimum is defined by the US Product Safety Commission, which states, "Stationary climbing equipment should have a use zone extending a minimum of 6 feet in all directions from the perimeter of the equipment." (Source: cpsc.gov/cpscpub/pubs/323.html.) This applies to playground equipment. Keep in mind that if you are doing dynos or have a steep overhang, you will need more than that. Additionally, you need floor space to assemble the wall. A reasonable floor workspace is about equal to the wall space the climbing wall will use.

Question: How many climbing holds should I buy?

Answer: If you use standard 8-inch spacing, there will be seventy-two holes per sheet of 4 x 8 plywood. You could get by with half that number. If you are just getting started, get thirty to forty holds. Expand your climbing hold collection over time.

Question: Why use ¾-inch plywood?

Answer: The reason you'd use ¾-inch plywood is to accommodate the thickness of the T nut. The T nut itself is ½ inch long. When the hold is tightened onto the wall, the T nut will pull into the back of the plywood. This will prevent the hold from tightening further. Yes, ½-inch plywood is strong enough to hold the weight of climbers.

So, if you really want to use ½-inch plywood, an option may be to use screw-on holds. There is a good variety of screw-on hand and foot holds available. Also, it is not difficult to make your own wooden screw-on holds. If you are on a budget, this is probably the way to go. You will save the cost of T nuts and holds and are able to use less-expensive plywood.

The thickness of a T nut is ¹⁄₂ inch; therefore you need to use ³⁄₄-inch plywood. The extra thickness is needed to allow the T nut to be pulled into the plywood as the hold is tightened, without the T nut contacting the hold.

Appendix B
Common Construction Terms

This is a small list including only the common construction terms that are most likely to be relevant to building a climbing wall.

aggregate: Sand, gravel, crushed stone, or rocks used to give strength to concrete. The particles of gravel and sand interlock and, together with cement, form a strong material called concrete.

anchor bolt: This is the bolt that securely attaches one climbing wall section to another. Usually anchor bolts are used to attach the bottom or top plates of a wall to the floor or ceiling. There are different types of anchor bolts. For concrete, use drop-in concrete expansion anchors. For a ceiling or wall ledger, use lag screws (some people call them lag bolts; however, they are technically a screw by definition).

architect: Someone trained and possessing a degree in architecture and certified to design public buildings and structures.

backing: A short piece of 2 x 4 added horizontally between studs or joists to provide an attachment point or to provide additional stability for plywood sheeting. See also blocking.

beam: A structural member that holds or supports the weight of other support members. Also called a girder.

bearing point: The specific spot where the weight is passed to another structural member or to the floor. Also called point load.

bearing wall: In home construction the wall that supports the ceiling joists or bears the weight of the structure above it.

bevel: An angled cut (not 90 degrees) along the edge of a member. A bevel cut would join two structural members along the sides, as compared to joining two structural members at their ends (using a miter cut). See also miter.

blocking: A short piece of 2 x 4 mounted vertically on a stud. If the sheet of plywood does not extend far enough to reach the stud, blocking can be added to provided additional attach points. See also backing.

bottom chord: When referring to a roof truss system, the bottom chord is the lower horizontal piece of the roof truss system. The bottom chord attaches to the walls.

bottom plate: The bottom horizontal piece of a framed wall. The studs of a wall are held in place with the top and bottom plates. See also top plate.

building code: A set of standards or ordinances, enforced by local laws, for the purpose of standardizing construction for safety and usability.

cement: The gray powder that is the "glue" in concrete.

chipboard: See oriented strand board (OSB).

concrete: A mixture of cement, aggregate, and water.

concrete block: An 8 x 8 x 16-inch block of concrete. They are poured in a form and are hollow to reduce weight.

concrete screw: A special screw made for fastening objects to concrete. By convention, concrete screws are painted blue. Concrete screws are also called masonry screws.

connector: See structural connectors.

continuous load path: A linking of each joint in a framing system from the top to the foundation. The force of weight is transferred through a structure to the foundation through a continuous load path.

drywall: See sheetrock.

drywall mud: See joint compound.

drywall screw: A short self-tapping screw used to attach drywall to studs.

fasteners: Anything used to connect or fasten framing members. For climbing walls the fasteners are screws and sometimes bolts. The bottom plates are fastened to the foundation with anchors. Nails are not used as fasteners for climbing walls.

fire block: Similar to backing, except the function is to prevent fire from spreading inside a framed wall. Also called fire stop.

fire stop: See fire block.

framing: The task of building the frame of a structure.

framing inspection: An inspection performed by an inspector from the city office responsible for enforcing codes and permits.

framing materials: The materials that make up wood-framed structures. A climbing wall is composed of studs, joists, top and bottom plates, trusses, and plywood sheathing or sheeting.

girder: A large structural member that supports other support members. Also called a beam.

inside corner: A corner that is less than 180 degrees.

joint: The point where two or more structural members are connected, or the line at which two sheets of plywood meet. Joints are strengthened by structural connectors.

joint cement: See joint compound.

joint compound: Used in drywall to cover the joints of sheetrock that form the walls and ceiling of a house. Also called joint cement or drywall mud.

joist: A horizontal framing member of a floor or ceiling. A joist's size commonly ranges from 2 x 6 inches to 2 x 12 inches. Joists are horizontal, whereas a stud is a vertical member of a wall. In climbing wall construction, due to the angled nature of the climbing surfaces, the distinction between a stud and a joist is not clear, and the term is often used interchangeably. See also stud.

joist hanger: A metal U-shaped bracket used to support the end of a floor joist and attached with hardened nails to another bearing joist or beam.

kick panel: A specific term used in home climbing wall construction that developed out of convention. It refers to the small vertical wall that lifts the inclined climbing wall off the floor level. Its purpose is to provide clearance for the crash pad. If not used, the first foot of the climbing wall would be unusable.

lag screw: Often called a lag bolt, it is a screw by definition. Lag screws have a hexagonal head for use with a wrench, and screw-type threads. Due to the large diameter of the shaft, a pilot hole should be drilled for installation of the lag screw. The hole should be the size of the shaft, allowing the screw threads to grip the wood.

ledger: A large wooden framing member used to transfer the load to a wall.

level: Horizontal with respect to the force of gravity. See also plumb.

manufactured wood: See oriented strand board (OSB).

masonry screw: See concrete screw.

miter: An angled joint of two pieces of wood. For example, a picture frame forms a 90-degree joint. The joints are formed by two pieces, each cut at 45 degrees. See also bevel.

on center (OC): Refers to the measurement and location of studs or joists. The measurement is taken from the center of one member to the center of the next.

oriented strand board (OSB): A 4 x 8-foot sheet of wood made by pressing and gluing wood chips together. This is less expensive than plywood; however, it should not be used in the construction of climbing walls. It is not as strong and is much heavier. It is sometimes called chipboard because of the chips that make up its composition.

outside corner: A corner that is greater than 180 degrees.

overhang: A structure with an angle less than vertical. Measured from horizontal to the wall surface, the resulting angle is less than 90 degrees.

particleboard: See oriented strand board (OSB).

permit: An authorization to proceed with new construction or modification of an existing facility or structure.

pilot hole: A hole into which a screw will be inserted. Usually pilot holes are used for large screws and lag screws. The pilot hole prevents the wood from splitting and reduces stress on the screw.

plan view: The top-down angle of view of a drawing.

plumb: Vertical with respect to the force of gravity. Perpendicular to level. See also level.

plywood: A panel made by pressing plies of wood veneer together at right angles to the grain. The layers are glued together in a stack to form a determined thickness. Due to the layering at right angles, plywood has a high shear strength. Three-quarter-inch plywood should be used for climbing walls.

point load: See bearing point.

portland cement: A type of cement composed of clay and limestone. When water and aggregate are added, it forms concrete.

post: A vertical framing member that usually completes the load path to the foundation or into the ground. Posts are usually 4 x 4 or 6 x 6 inches in size.

pressure-treated wood: Structural members that have been infused with a preservative. Pressure-treated wood will withstand the elements longer than untreated wood. However, a preservative can be added to untreated wood after framing.

primer: The coat of material applied to bare wood. Primer is not paint. Primer is designed to adhere to the wood and provide a bonding surface for paint.

primer-sealer: A type of primer that also has water-sealing properties. In addition to providing a bonding surface for paint, it seals moisture out.

sheathing: See sheeting.

sheeting: The plywood panel that is fastened to studs or joists. The sheeting forms the climbing surface of a climbing wall. Climbing holds are mounted to the sheeting. Also called sheathing.

sheetrock: A 4 x 8-foot panel composed of gypsum sandwiched between a thick paper. Sheetrock is used in construction to form the finished walls of a house.

structural connectors: Hardware that connects the individual structural members of a climbing wall together. Structural connectors increase the strength of a joint. Structural connectors are available in many shapes designed to fit common joints found in framing. For more information about structural connectors, see Structural Connectors under step 4 in chapter 2.

stud: A vertical framing member of a wall held in place by top and bottom plates. Studs are typically 2 x 4 inches in size; however, larger studs can be used to form thicker walls. In climbing wall construction, due to the angled nature of the climbing surfaces, the distinction between a stud and a joist is not clear, and the term is often used interchangeably. See also joist.

tie plate: A flat metal plate with holes for screws used to reinforce a flat surface joint.

tie strap: A flat metal strap. For use in climbing wall construction, it may be used in a similar way as a tie plate. A tie strap may be chosen over a tie plate due to its more convenient size.

top plate: The top horizontal piece of a framed wall. The studs of a wall are held in place with the top and bottom plates.

treated wood: See pressure-treated wood.

water-repellent preservative: A liquid applied to wood to give the wood water-repellent properties. See also pressure-treated wood.

wood screw: A self-tapping screw designed to attach two wood members together.

Appendix C
Climbing Terms

aid climbing: This form of climbing is most often used for climbing high, towering walls. Anchors are placed or drilled into the rock with slings and stirrups attached. The climber uses the placed anchors directly for climbing.

approach: The path taken, usually over difficult terrain such as a boulder field or brush, to reach the base of a climbing route.

approach shoes: Special shoes that blend the characteristics of hiking shoes and climbing shoes. They are usually made with a sticky rubber sole for traction on steeper grades of rock and rock scrambling. Used by climbers while approaching the climbing location.

arête: An outward-facing, V-shaped ridge found on a climbing route.

auto belay: This device attaches to the top of an artificial wall and is used to provide automated toprope climbing protection. The device works via a small governor that limits the speed of rope travel. The climber can climb up or down with a slight tension on the rope. However, if the climber falls, the faster rope travel engages the governor and the speed of travel is maintained at a constant, safe rate.

back clipping: When the rope is traveling toward the climber in the same direction as the gate of the carabiner, it is considered back clipping. For example, if the climber is up and to the right of the protection, and the gate of the quickdraw is facing to the right, and the rope runs from the belayer into the carabiner toward the wall, then on up to the climber, this is back clipping.

The gate should face left if the climber is to the right of the protection, and the rope should enter the carabiner from the belayer on the wall side and exit on the side of the carabiner away from the wall. The reason for this is that under some circumstances during a fall, the rope may press across the outside of the gate, causing the gate to open.

backstep: Performed with the hip turned sideways to the wall while one foot steps backwards.

barn door: When the frame of a door is tipped, the door will swing. In the same way, when a climber has his weight shifted off vertical and only has two points of contact with the wall, he will swing uncontrollably away from the wall.

belay: To protect a roped climber from falling by passing the rope through or around any type of friction-enhancing belay device. Before belay devices were invented, the rope was simply passed around the belayer's hips to create friction.

belay device: The purpose of a belay device is to help the belayer lock the rope when necessary and allow the belayer to give out rope when needed. There are many belay devices, each providing a special advantage for different types of climbing.

"Belay off!": When belayers remove their belays, they call "Belay off!" This is to notify the climber that he is no longer protected by belay. This should be called every time, whether or not the climber and belayer are in sight of each other.

"Belay on!": When belayers place climbers on belays, they call "Belay on!" This notifies climbers they are on belay and may now begin climbing.

belay station: The location of the belayer. It can be designated in an indoor climbing gym, or established during an ascent on a rock face or ledge. An outdoor belay station is set up with a minimum of two anchor points connected with webbing. (Three or more anchor points would provide better backup protection in the event of failure of one of the anchors.) The webbing has a locking carabiner in the middle that the object being anchored is attached to.

beta: Giving advice, hints between climbers. Applies to all types of climbing.

bouldering: A style of climbing without ropes that is popular outdoors and in indoor climbing gyms. In addition to a crash pad, a spotter stands ready to guide a falling boulderer to land on the mat safely. Bouldering is usually limited to low heights where a climber can take a fall without injury (other than to his pride).

bucket: A large and deep handhold. It may refer to a natural feature on an outdoor route or to an indoor climbing hold.

buildering: Bouldering on buildings.

bump: Moving to the final hold using another hold in one smooth motion.

campus board: A set of horizontal rungs placed about 8 inches apart vertically. It is used to practice and train upper body, arm, and finger strength. To campus, the climber places both hands on one campus rung. She performs a pull-up, then reaches up with a hand to the other rung while continuing the pull-up motion. Then the other hand reaches up to the next rung, and so on. An alternative to this can be done with two hands on the same rung, pulling up, then quickly snapping both hands up to the next rung, then repeating.

campusing: Climbing without using feet. The feet do not touch the wall at all.

carabiner, locking carabiner: These are gated devices used to attach a rope to a fixed anchor or to tie into protection points. The gate is on a spring-loaded hinge, and may be nonlocking or locking.

chalk: This is simply magnesium carbonate, or $MgCO_3$. Chalk is used to keep a climber's hands dry. Stress and exertion make hands sweat. Sweat reduces friction. Chalk reduces the moisture and helps improve friction between the hands and climbing holds.

chalk bag: Used to store chalk while climbing. Chalk bags strap around the waist and hang at the back at about tailbone height. Usually chalk bags have some type of closure so the chalk won't spill when not in use.

chimney: A formation where three sides form a U shape and are vertical and parallel. The chimney is climbed by applying opposing pressure to the sides and back.

"Climbing!": The climber calls "Climbing!" then waits for the "Climb on!" reply from the belayer before beginning the climb.

climbing harness: A harness is used by a belayer to fasten him to the anchor point, and by the climber to fasten him to the rope. A climbing harness consists of a belt with leg loops, gear loops, and anchor point.

climbing helmet: Protects the climber from falling rock and from impact in the event of a fall. Climbing helmets are unique. They have an outer hard plastic shell and an inner shell fitted for comfort. Do not use bicycle helmets or other types of helmets. Some helmets are designed to break away during impact. Climbing helmets are designed to remain fastened to the head since climbers may experience multiple impacts with the wall before the rope arrests the fall. Climbing helmets must meet the

US government standard EN 12492, Snell N-94.

climbing holds: Used for climbing artificial climbing walls. Holds are attached to a climbing wall by bolt or screw. They are available in many colors, shapes, and textures and are sold commercially by many companies.

climbing rope: Climbing ropes are designed to catch a climber in the event of a fall and to absorb the force of a fall by stretching. The degree to which a rope stretches is its dynamic quality. Climbing ropes should stretch a little with a sudden impact force.

climbing shoes: Special shoes for rock climbing and indoor climbing that have a unique sticky rubber sole, heel, and toe.

"Climb on!": The belayer calls "Climb on!" after hearing the climber call "Climbing!" This signifies to the climber that the belayer is actively belaying.

clip stick: A stick, such as a broom handle or extendable roller pole (for painting) with a quickdraw taped to the end. Sometimes the gate of the top carabiner is held open by some temporary object that will fall away when the carabiner is clipped. The other (lower) carabiner has the climbing rope passed through it. The stick with quickdraw is lifted to the first protection and clipped in. This allows protection to be placed over a dangerous start.

competition climbing: Sometimes abbreviated by climbers and called "comp." These are fun, friendly, organized competitions held at indoor climbing gyms. There are three main categories of climbing competition: difficulty, bouldering, and speed. The difficulty comps are further subdivided into redpoint, on sight, and flash. See indoorclimbing.com/comp_types.html for more information.

crack climbing: The art of climbing up a crack without other hand or foot holds.

crag: Slang for a local climbing area.

crash pad: A mat used to break the fall when bouldering. Used with a spotter, the crash pad reduces the risk of injury from a fall.

crimp: A technique of gripping a hold, where the fingertips press flat on an edge or ridge with the thumb pressing on top of the fingernails. The first knuckle is bent toward the body, and the second knuckle is bent toward the wall.

crimper: A small hold wide enough for three or four fingers.

crossover: A climbing movement where one arm crosses over the other while reaching for the next hold.

crux: The most difficult place on the route. Usually a route setter will only place one crux. The crux should only be one-half to one grade higher than the overall rating of the climb.

dead hang: A training routine where the climber hangs straight down without feet touching for as long as possible.

dead point: A climbing movement where a hold is grasped at the moment of weightlessness at the top of a dynamic move.

dihedral: Depending on the context, it could describe a rock feature in which two vertical rock faces meet, forming a vertical corner or ridge. It may also refer to a geometric term describing the intersection of two planes. In the context of building your own climbing wall, the climbing wall builder may design two climbing surfaces to meet at differing angles. The joint between two angled plywood climbing surfaces is the dihedral angle. If two vertically angled climbing surfaces protrude, they form a feature that climbers call a dihedral.

kneedrop: One knee is lowered by rotating the hips right or left.

dyno: A dynamic movement to reach a higher set of holds, where momentum is used to propel the body.

edging: Using the edge of the climbing shoe on a tiny ridge.

face climbing: Climbing a near vertical face. This type of climbing requires balance and precision. Usually there are no holds that allow a full grip.

features: These are the ridges, bumps, pockets, protrusions, etc. that give an otherwise flat surface contours.

figure four: In cases where there is no foothold and the next handhold is just out of reach, a little extension of reach can be gained by putting the leg over the opposite forearm and pressing down with the legs. This allows the hold to be pressed down to the hip level, something that could not be done with just arm strength alone, and thus gives an extra 6 to 8 inches of reach to the unused hand.

finger board: Sometimes confused with a campus board. This is a training device with small, finger-size pockets or ridges that is used to improve finger and grip strength. It can be placed above door jambs and at other convenient locations.

flagging: A foot technique where the leg is extended to maintain balance. It is placed against the wall with slight pressure.

flapper, bloody flapper: A common minor type of injury for climbers where the skin lifts up in a flap. Climbers use tape on their fingertips to prevent flappers and/or to hold them in place.

flash: Climbing a route on the first attempt. A climber may watch another climber complete the route, or may receive beta prior to climbing.

floor anchor: In indoor climbing, an anchor on the floor designates the belay location. The belayer anchors into the floor anchor separately from the belay system attaching the climber. If the climber falls, the belayer is held by the floor anchor, preventing him from being pulled up into the air by the force of the climber's fall.

friction: This is the traction received from surface-to-surface contact. Usually a friction climb is done on sloping inclines. Sometimes steep inclines with small holds use a combination of pockets, crimpers, and friction.

gaston: A type of grip using sideways pressure on the hold. The thumb points down and the elbow points out.

hand jam: A technique used with cracks in which the climber gains friction from the interior of the crack. This is done by "jamming" the hand into the crack, then twisting the hand and/or clenching the fist. The twisting and clenching creates a tight jam.

hand traverse: Moving in a horizontal direction using handholds and smearing.

heel hook: Performed by latching the heel over a hold and pulling upward with the legs. This movement takes weight off the arms, allowing one arm to pull up and lock off, freeing the other arm to reach for a hold.

indoor climbing: Developed in the 1980s using wooden protrusions nailed to a wall, indoor climbing has evolved into its own dynamic sport. As of 2012 there were about 3,000 climbing gyms worldwide.

jib: A small foothold.

jug: A large, full-hand-size hold.

layback: Usually performed on a crack or sidepull hold. Weight is supported by sideways pulling, while the feet provide opposing pressure.

lead climbing: The process of ascending a climb with the rope. The lead climber ascends and clips the rope through preset quickdraws. At the top the rope is passed through the final anchor and the climber is lowered to the ground

lock-off: Locking the arm in close to the chest, at about a 45-degree angle. A lock-off seems to use less energy than attempting to hold a more open angle.

mantle: A movement used to climb over a ledge or large round surface. Mantling uses friction with palms down on the rock.

match hands/match feet: Both hands or feet use the same hold. Typically done as a transition movement, usually one hand or foot is on top of the other, while the bottom hand or foot slips out, leaving the top hand or foot on the hold and the previous bottom hand or foot free to move to the next hold.

mono: A type of hold that has a hole just large enough for a single finger.

nub, nubbin: These are very small protrusions, usually only usable as a foothold.

off-width crack: This refers to a crack size that is too wide to be used with a hand jam, but too small to fit the body into to use as a chimney.

on sight: (1.) A climbing competition format. The competitor is allowed to preview the route, then returns to isolation until called to climb. No beta or watching other competitors is allowed in this format. (2.) A term used to describe a climber's successful completion of a lead route without previous knowledge or beta.

overhang: A wall face that is inclined overhead or beyond vertical. A negative angle is overhung. A positive angle is a slab. See also slab.

peel: Falling abruptly from a wall, either outdoors or indoors.

pendulum: This happens when climbing an overhang with a toprope. If the climber falls, the rope catches the climber and swings him out, away from the wall. This can also happen on a lead climb if the climber has just completed clipping in above his position, then falls.

pumped: If a climber overuses his grip, lactic acid builds up. The forearms bulge and feel tight. This results in loss of grip strength. A climber may say he is pumped, meaning he has nothing left in the grip.

quickdraw: Two carabiners attached together with a web runner form a quickdraw. The function of a quickdraw is to let the rope travel more freely and to reduce the chance of twisting the carabiner in an anchor point.

rappel: Using a rope and descending device to abseil down the face of a cliff.

rappelling gloves: Special gloves that allow freedom of movement and dexterity while protecting the hands from friction while rapelling.

redpoint: Successful completion of a climb following one or more unsuccessful attempts, or after first practicing sections of the route.

rock scrambling: A level of climbing where both hands and feet are used. More difficult than hiking, but less difficult than climbing.

rope bag: A specially designed haul bag for the climbing rope. There are many different features available depending on a climber's type of climbing and personal taste. Rope bags provide protection for the rope and make it easy to transport and access the rope for use without tangling.

route: A set of holds placed by a route setter. Routes are marked, named, and graded.

runner: A nylon tubular material used for slings, and combined with carabiners to make quickdraws.

screw-on holds: Usually smaller than a standard climbing hold. Rather than bolt in using a T nut and bolt, these holds screw onto the plywood. They are usually used for footholds. However, large screw-on holds are available and work well.

sewing machine leg: When anxiety and stress build up, muscles tend to shake. When a climber extends his leg to the next hold and begins to place a little pressure on the calves, the muscles shake a little. By pressing a little harder, putting a little more tension on the calf muscles, the shaking will stop. New climbers don't know this, so the natural reaction is to place less pressure on the foothold. The shaking itself causes more anxiety and leads to more shaking.

sidepull: A type of climbing hold that is intended by the route setter to be used with sideways pressure. The difference between this and a gaston is that a gaston is done in front of the body, with thumb down and elbow out. A sidepull may be out to the side of the body with thumb up.

sit-start: This is a common starting position for a climb. The climber sits and places feet on the starting footholds and grasps the handholds, then lifts himself off the ground to begin climbing.

slab: A low-angle incline face. Slabs are usually flat and featureless, but they may have small jibs. A slab is a positive incline.

sloper: A type of hold that is smooth and usually large enough to require the climber to use friction along the palm and fingers.

smear: Placing the foot directly on the rock where there are no obvious holds and gaining purchase solely from the friction between the shoe and rock (no pun intended).

smearing: Performed by placing the flat surface of the shoe's sole on a smooth rock face.

sport climbing: Usually refers to outdoor climbing with fixed protection on named routes. Sport climbing developed from traditional climbing but is now its own form of the sport.

spotter: When bouldering, the climber may break loose and fall unexpectedly. The spotter breaks the fall and guides the fall to the mat, reducing the chance of injury to the boulderer.

static movement: Placing hands or feet without using momentum. Usually the body and other three limbs remain static while the moving limb is placed on the next hold.

stemming: Widely spaced foot placements, usually on faces forming a V or valley.

step-through: A climbing movement where one leg crosses in front of the other while stepping to the next hold.

technical climbing: This is a general term describing the techniques and equipment used while climbing with ropes. A pair or team of climbers use specialized equipment, clothing, and ropes to scale a rock face.

T nut: A type of nut that has a T shape. The flat, T part of the nut pulls into the plywood by the bolt. It usually has small barbs that prevent the nut from turning as the bolt tightens. A T nut is ideal for mounting climbing holds to plywood.

toprope: A common style of climbing in indoor climbing gyms. The rope goes from the belayer to the top of the route, over a bar, then down to the climber. This gives the climber the best protection and least distance to fall.

trad climbing: This type of climbing differs from other forms of climbing by the way the climber places protection. "Trad" is short for traditional and is the original style of technical climbing. Cams, nuts, and sometimes pitons are wedged into cracks. A carabiner and runner connect to the protection. The rope runs through a carabiner on the loose end of the runner.

traverse: Climbing across the wall horizontally, rather than up the wall.

undercling: Orientation of a climbing hold so that the most positive grip is on the lower side of the hold.

woodie: One of the original slang names given to a home climbing wall. A home wall is typically made of wood rather than rock, thus the name "woodie."

Yosemite Decimal System: Also referred to as YDS. The YDS incorporates ratings for hiking (Class 1), cross-country trekking (Class 2), rock scrambling (Class 3), steep terrain such as mountaineering using ropes but not protection (Class 4), and technical rock climbing (Class 5). The scale for technical climbing ranges from 5.0 up to about 5.16. A 5.0 climb would use ropes and protection, but the hand and foot holds would be very large, such as a mountain with large stair-step rocks, yet steep enough and high enough to require protection. A 5.6 rating might be something you would find on a children's wall at an indoor climbing gym with holds larger than several inches in diameter. The wall might be vertical or with a positive incline. A 5.9 climb might be upper intermediate level. The rating increases up to about 5.16, which is extremely difficult and achievable by just a few of the most elite climbers. **Note:** The decimal in the YDS rating should be thought of like a dash "-", so you increase from five-nine to five-ten to five-eleven, and so on. If it were thought of as a number it might appear that 5.10 and 5.1 are the same, or that 5.9 is higher than 5.16, which is not the case.

Z-clipping: When lead climbing, the climber must grab the rope between the harness and the last clip (usually a quickdraw) and lift it to the next clip. With Z-clipping the climber incorrectly grabs the rope on the other side of the clip (going to the belayer). This causes a Z clip, forming what looks like a Z. This mistake usually happens when the protection is placed close together. It is dangerous because it may cause the carabiner gate to twist against the rope and open. The most common problem is the excessive rope drag it causes.

Appendix D
Rise-Run Chart

Measure the height of your interior walls. Decide what angle you want your climbing wall to be. Find the applicable ceiling height, then the desired angle. To the right of the desired angle is the "run." The run is the distance from the wall on the ceiling where the climbing wall will be anchored. When anchored to the floor at the base of the wall, it will create the desired inclined angle.

Your Ceiling Height	→	Your Desired Angle	→	Look up "Run"

	Desired Angle	In Inches Run is:	In Centimeters Run is:
7 feet **213.6 cm** Ceiling Height	5	7 3/8	18.7
	10	14 3/4	37.6
	15	22 1/2	57.2
	20	30 1/2	77.7
	25	39 1/8	99.5
	30	48 1/2	123.2
	35	58 7/8	149.4
	40	70 1/2	179.0
	45	84	213.4
8 feet **243.8 cm** Ceiling Height	5	8 3/8	21.3
	10	17	43.0
	15	25 3/4	65.3
	20	35	88.8
	25	44 3/4	113.7
	30	55 1/2	140.8
	35	67 1/4	170.7
	40	80 1/2	204.6
	45	96	243.8

Your Ceiling Height	→	Your Desired Angle	→	Look up "Run"

	Desired Angle	In Inches Run is:	In Centimeters Run is:
	5	9 1/2	24.0
	10	19	48.4
	15	29	73.5
	20	39 1/4	99.8
9 feet	25	50 3/8	127.9
274.3 cm	30	62 1/4	158.4
Ceiling Height	35	75 5/8	192.1
	40	90 1/2	230.2
	45	108	274.3
	5	10 1/2	26.7
	10	21 1/4	53.7
	15	32 1/8	81.7
	20	43 3/4	110.9
10 feet	25	56	142.1
304.8 cm	30	69 1/4	176.0
Ceiling Height	35	84	213.4
	40	100 3/4	255.8
	45	120	304.8

| Your Ceiling Height | → | Your Desired Angle | → | Look up "Run" |

	Desired Angle	In Inches Run is:	In Centimeters Run is:
	5	11 1/2	29.3
	10	23 1/4	59.1
	15	35 3/8	89.8
	20	48	122.0
11 feet	25	61 1/2	156.3
335.3 cm	30	76 1/4	193.6
Ceiling Height	35	92 3/8	234.8
	40	110 3/4	281.3
	45	132	335.3
	5	12 5/8	32.0
	10	25 1/2	64.5
	15	38 5/8	98.0
	20	52 1/2	133.1
12 feet	25	67 1/8	170.6
365.8 cm	30	83 1/4	211.2
Ceiling Height	35	100 7/8	256.1
	40	120 3/4	306.9
	45	144	365.8

Index

About
the Author

Steve Lage is owner and webmaster of Indoorclimbing.com and manages the website full time. His interest in climbing began back in 1976 as he was just starting an Air Force career. While stationed at the Air Force Academy in Colorado Springs, Colorado, he and his Air Force buddies would slip off to the Garden of the Gods for rock climbing every chance they got.

He continued in the Air Force and was assigned to civil engineering as an engineering assistant. While on active duty he completed his degree in computer science at Chapman University. At about that same time, the new sport of indoor climbing was emerging. In 1998 he used his engineering experience and computer knowledge to provide the first online source for how to build a home climbing wall. He

Author Steve Lage hikes near the Grand Canyon.

has personally built several home climbing walls, including those featured in this book, and he spearheaded the approval and construction of a racquetball conversion climbing gym while stationed in Germany. Steve retired from the Air Force following a thirty-year career. He remains active in many outdoor pursuits. He especially enjoys day hiking, camping, and outdoor and indoor climbing.

PROTECTING CLIMBING **ACCESS** SINCE 1991

ACCESS FUND

| JOIN US |
WWW.ACCESSFUND.ORG